Here's what people are saying about
the DOING LIFE TOGETHER *Series . . .*

Small Group Members Are Saying . . .

Six weeks ago we were strangers. Today we are a family in Christ. We talk to each other, lean on each other, encourage each other, and hold each other accountable. We have gone from meeting as a Bible study to getting together for several social events, meeting for Sunday services, and organizing service projects in our community.

—Sandy and Craig

The Purpose-Driven material quickly moved us beyond group and closer toward family, beyond reading God's Word to knowing God!

—The Coopers

Small Group Leaders Are Saying . . .

Even though our group has been together for several years, the questions in this study have allowed us to connect on a much deeper level. Many of the men are displaying emotions we haven't seen before.

—Steve and Jennifer

The material has become a personal compass to me. When I find myself needing to make a decision, I ask, "Does it bring me closer to God's family? Does it make me more like Christ? Am I using the gifts God gave me? Am I sharing God's love? Am I surrendering my life to please God?" I still have a long way to go, but this has been a blessing and a compass to keep me on his path.

—Craig

Pastors and Church Leaders Are Saying . . .

We took the entire church through this curriculum, and the results were nothing less than miraculous. Our congregation was ignited with passion for God and his purposes for our lives. It warmed up the entire congregation as we grew closer to God by "Doing Life Together."

—Kerry

The Purpose-Driven format helped our groups realize there are some areas that they are doing very well in (fellowship and discipleship) and other areas that they need to do some work in. What is amazing is to see how they are committing to work on these areas (especially evangelism and ministry).

—Steve

Other Studies in the DOING LIFE TOGETHER Series

Beginning Life Together (God's Purposes for Your Life)

Connecting with God's Family (Fellowship)

Developing Your SHAPE to Serve Others (Ministry)

Sharing Your Life Mission Every Day (Evangelism)

Surrendering Your Life for God's Pleasure (Worship)

After you complete this study, we'd love to hear how DOING LIFE TOGETHER has affected your life, your group, or your church! Write us at stories@lifetogether.com. You can also log on to www.lifetogether.com to see how others are putting "life together" into practice.

GROWING TO BE LIKE CHRIST

six sessions on
discipleship

written by
BRETT and DEE EASTMAN
TODD and DENISE WENDORFF
KAREN LEE-THORP

GRAND RAPIDS, MICHIGAN 49530 USA

We want to hear from you. Please send your comments about this book to us in care of the address below. Thank you.

GRAND RAPIDS, MICHIGAN 49530 USA

WWW.ZONDERVAN.COM

ZONDERVAN™

Growing to Be Like Christ

Requests for information should be addressed to:

Zondervan, *Grand Rapids, Michigan 49530*

ISBN 0-310-24674-1

Interior icons by Tom Clark

Printed in the United States of America

09 10 • 30 29 28

CONTENTS

FOREWORD

Over twenty-five years ago I noticed a little phrase in Acts 13:36 that forever altered the direction of my life. It read, *"David had served God's purpose in his own generation."* I was fascinated by that simple yet profound summary of David's life, and I determined to make it the goal of my life, too. I would seek to discover and fulfill the purposes for which God had created me.

This decision provoked a number of questions: What are God's purposes for putting us on earth? What does a purpose-driven life look like? How can the church enable people to fulfill God's eternal purposes? I read through the Bible again and again, searching for the answers to these questions. As a direct result of what I learned, my wife, Kay, and I decided to start Saddleback Church and build it from the ground up on God's five purposes for us (which are found in the New Testament).

In the living laboratory of Saddleback Church, we were able to experiment with different ways to help people understand, apply, and live out the purposes of God. I've written two books about the lessons we've learned (*The Purpose-Driven Church* and, more recently, *The Purpose-Driven Life*). As other churches became interested in what we were doing, we began sharing the tools, programs, and studies we developed at Saddleback. Over a million copies of *The Purpose-Driven Church* are now in print in some nineteen languages, and The Purpose-Driven Class Curriculum (Class 101–401) is now used in tens of thousands of churches around the world. We hope that the same will be true for this exciting new small group curriculum.

DOING LIFE TOGETHER is a groundbreaking study in several ways. It is the first small group curriculum built completely on the purpose-driven paradigm. This is not just another study to be used *in* your church; it is a study *on* the church to help *strengthen* your church. Many small group curricula today are quite self-focused and individualistic. They generally do not address the importance of the local church and our role in it as believers. Another unique feature of this curriculum is its balance. In every session, the five purposes of God are stressed in some way.

But the greatest reason I am excited about releasing this DOING LIFE TOGETHER curriculum is that I've seen the dramatic changes it produces in the lives of those who study it. These small group studies were not developed in some detached ivory tower or academic setting but in the day-to-day ministry of Saddleback Church, where thousands of people meet weekly in small groups that are committed to fulfilling God's purposes. This curriculum has been tested and retested, and the results have been absolutely amazing. Lives have been changed, marriages saved, and families strengthened. And our church has grown—in the past seven years we've seen over 9,100 new believers baptized at Saddleback. I attribute these results to the fact that so many of our members are serious about living healthy, balanced, purpose-driven lives.

It is with great joy and expectation that I introduce this resource to you. I am so proud of our development team on this project: Brett and Dee Eastman, Todd and Denise Wendorff, and Karen Lee-Thorp. They have committed hundreds of hours to write, teach, develop, and refine these lessons —with much feedback along the way. This has been a labor of love, as they have shared our dream of helping you serve God's purpose in your own generation. The church will be enriched for eternity as a result.

Get ready for a life-changing journey. God bless!

—Pastor Rick Warren

Pastor Rick Warren is the author of *The Purpose-Driven Church* and *The Purpose-Driven Life* [www.purposedrivenlife.com].

ACKNOWLEDGMENTS

Sometimes in life God gives you a dream. Most of the time it remains only a dream. But every once in a while, a dream captures your heart, consumes your thoughts, and compels you to action. However, if others around you aren't motivated to share the dream and aren't moved to action along with you, it remains just that—a dream. By the grace of God and a clear call on the hearts of a few, our dream has become a reality.

The DOING LIFE TOGETHER series was birthed one summer in the hearts of Brett and Dee Eastman and Todd and Denise Wendorff, two Saddleback Church staff couples. They hoped to launch a new one-year Bible study based on the Purpose-Driven® life. They called it *The Journey: Experiencing the Transformed Life*. *The Journey* was launched with a leadership team that committed its heart and soul to the project. We will never be able to express our gratitude to each of you who shared the dream and helped to continue the dream now, three years later.

Early on, Karen Lee-Thorp, an experienced writer of many Bible studies, joined the team. Oh, God, you are good to us!

Saddleback pastors and staff members too numerous to mention have supported our dream and have come alongside to fan the flames. We would have never gotten this off the ground without their belief and support.

We also want to express our overwhelming gratitude to the numerous ministries and churches that helped shape our spiritual heritage. We're particularly grateful for Bill Bright of Campus Crusade for Christ, who gave us a dream for reaching the world, and for Bill Hybels of Willow Creek Community Church, who gave us a great love and respect for the local church.

Our special thanks goes to Pastor Rick and Kay Warren for sharing the dream of a healthy and balanced purpose-driven church that produces purpose-driven lives over time. It clearly is the basis for the body of this work. God only knows how special you are to us and how blessed we feel to be a part of your team.

Finally, we thank our beloved families who have lived with us, laughed at us, and loved us through it all. We love doing our lives together with you.

READ ME FIRST

DOING LIFE TOGETHER

Doing Life Together is unique in that it was designed in community for community. Four of us have been doing life together, in one way or another, for over fifteen years. We have been in a small group together, done ministry together, and been deeply involved in each other's lives. We have shared singleness, marriage, childbirth, family loss, physical ailments, teenage years, job loss, and, yes, even marital problems.

Our community has not been perfect, but it has been real. We have made each other laugh beyond belief, cry to the point of exhaustion, feel as grateful as one can imagine, and get so mad we couldn't see straight. We've said things we will always regret and shared moments we will never forget, but through it all we have discovered a diamond in the rough—a community that increasingly reflects the character of Jesus Christ. God has used our relationships with each other to deepen our understanding of and intimacy with him. We have come to believe that we cannot fully experience the breadth and depth of the purpose-driven life outside of loving relationships in the family of God (Ephesians 2:19–22; 4:11–13).

Doing life together was God's plan from the beginning of time. From the relationships of Father, Son, and Holy Spirit in the Trinity, to the twelve apostles, to the early house churches, and even Jesus' final words in the Great Commission (Matthew 28:16–20)—all share the pattern of life together. God longs to connect all of his children in loving relationships that cultivate the five biblical purposes of the church deep within their hearts. With this goal in mind, we have created the Doing Life Together series—the first purpose-driven small group series.

The series is designed to walk you and your group down a path, six weeks at a time over the course of a year, to help you do the purpose-driven life together. There are six study guides in this series. You can study them individually, or you can follow the one-year path through the six studies. *Beginning Life Together* offers a six-week overview of the purpose-driven life. The other five guides (*Connecting with God's Family*, *Growing to Be Like Christ*, *Developing Your SHAPE to Serve Others*, *Sharing Your Life Mission Every Day*, and *Surrendering Your Life for God's Pleasure*) each explore one of the five purposes of the church more deeply.

In his book *The Purpose-Driven Life*, Rick Warren invites you to commit to live a purpose-driven life every day. The DOING LIFE TOGETHER series was designed to help you live this purpose-driven life through being part of a purpose-driven small group. A purpose-driven group doesn't simply connect people in community or grow people through Bible study. These groups seek to help each member balance all five biblical purposes of the church. The fivefold purpose of a healthy group parallels the fivefold purpose of the church.

What Is Spiritual Growth?

It's been said that success in your Christian life is to live each day as though Jesus Christ were in your place. We have just one problem with this definition. Most of the time, *we* want that place! After all, it's ours. It reminds us of standing in a long line and having somebody ask to go in front of us and take our place. On the outside we tell Jesus, "Sure, no problem," but inside we're saying "Are you crazy? Fat chance! This is *my* place, *my* life!" Let's be honest: growing in this way isn't easy.

Our experience, after a combined one hundred years of trying to let Jesus live his life through us, is that this can be elusive, hard work at times. Our desire is good, but doing it consistently is sometimes a struggle. Each of us on our team has gone up and down, but ultimately we have learned a few things along the way.

First of all, growing to be like Christ can be incredibly gratifying. Second, it's a *lifetime* transformation, not a quick fix. Third, it rarely happens consistently on our own—that's why we do it *together*.

People tell us that the number-one benefit they've received from going through the DOING LIFE TOGETHER series has been that they have grown in their walk with God. The six sessions in *Growing to Be Like Christ* will help you not only grow in understanding but also in experiencing a deeper walk with the Father.

Our motto is "Take Another Step." Each session is designed to encourage a small step in your walk with God. Paul said, "He who began a good work in you will carry it on to completion until the day of Christ Jesus" (Philippians 1:6). Our prayer for you is that he who began a good work in you will be faithful to complete it. We hope that at the end of these six sessions you will be more eager to let Jesus take his place in your life as time goes on.

Outline of Each Session

Most people desire to live a purpose-driven life, but few people actually achieve this on a consistent basis. That's why we've included elements of all five purposes in every meeting—so that you can live a healthy, balanced spiritual life over time.

When you see the following symbols in this book, you will know that the questions and exercises in that section promote that particular purpose.

CONNECTING WITH GOD'S FAMILY (FELLOWSHIP). The foundation for spiritual growth is an intimate connection with God and his family. The questions in this section will help you get to know the members of your small group so that you'll begin to feel a sense of belonging. This section is designed to open your time together and provide a fun way to share your personal stories with one another.

GROWING TO BE LIKE CHRIST (DISCIPLESHIP). This is the most exciting portion of each lesson. Each week you'll study one or two core passages from the Bible. The focus will be on how the truths from God's Word make a difference in your lives. We will often provide an experiential exercise to enable you not just to talk about the truth but also to experience it in a practical way.

DEVELOPING YOUR SHAPE TO SERVE OTHERS (MINISTRY). Most people want to know how God has uniquely shaped them for ministry and where they can serve in the center of his will. This section will help make that desire a reality. Every other week or so you will be encouraged to take practical steps in developing who God uniquely made you to be in order to serve him and others better.

SHARING YOUR LIFE MISSION EVERY DAY (EVANGELISM). Many people skip over this aspect of the Christian life because it's scary, relationally awkward, or simply too much work for their busy schedules. We understand, because we have these thoughts as well. But God calls all of us to reach out a hand to people who don't know him. It's much easier to take practical, manageable steps that can be integrated naturally into everyday life if you take them together. Every other week or so you will have an opportunity to take a small step.

SURRENDERING YOUR LIFE FOR GOD'S PLEASURE (WORSHIP). A surrendered heart is what pleases God most. Each small group session will give you a chance to surrender your heart to God and one another in prayer. In addition, you'll be introduced to several forms of small group worship, including listening to worship CDs, singing together, reading psalms, and participating in Communion. This portion of your meeting will transform your life in ways you never thought possible. If you're new to praying in a small group, you won't be pressed to pray aloud until you feel ready.

STUDY NOTES. This section provides background notes on the Bible passage(s) you examine in the GROWING section. You may want to refer to these notes during your study.

FOR FURTHER STUDY. This section can help your more spiritually mature members take the session one step further each week on their own. If your group is ready for deeper study or is comfortable doing homework, this section and the following two sections will help you get there. You may want to encourage them to read these passages and reflect on them in a personal journal or in the Notes section at the end of each session.

MEMORY VERSES. For those group members who want to take a step of hiding God's Word in their hearts, there are six memory verses on page 82 that correspond to each weekly lesson. You may want to tear out this page and cut the verses into wallet- or purse-size cards for easy access.

PURPOSE-DRIVEN LIFE READING PLAN. This plan for reading *The Purpose-Driven Life* by Rick Warren parallels the weekly sessions in this study guide. *The Purpose-Driven Life* is the perfect complement to the DOING LIFE TOGETHER series. If your group wants to apply the material taught in the book, you can simply read the recommended piece each week, write a reflection, and discuss the teaching as a group or in pairs.

DAILY DEVOTIONS. One of the easiest ways for your group to grow together is to encourage each other to read God's Word on a regular basis. It's so much easier to stay motivated in this area if you have one another's support. On page 83 is a daily reading plan that parallels the study and helps you deepen your walk with God. There are five readings per week. If you really want to grow, we suggest you pair up with a friend (spiritual partner) to encourage each other throughout the week. Decide right now, and write the name of someone you'd like to join with for the next six weeks.

SESSION 1

GROWING DEEPER IN CHRIST

Recently Dee asked me to run a half marathon with her—a race that would take place in a few months. Although I wanted so much to run the race with her, experience the excitement of being in a marathon, and spend time with her, my initial answer to her was no. I went home thinking about why. Why didn't I want to run this race? Eventually the reason became clear: I wasn't willing to do what it would take beforehand to run the race well. I wasn't willing to pay the cost of time and training in my schedule. I have other priorities that are more important to me.

I face the same decision every day in my spiritual life. If I really want to know Jesus Christ intimately, it takes time, energy, and the decision to let the Holy Spirit be in control of my life. Frankly, there are many days when I don't feel like sweating that hard! The only reason I drag out those spiritual running shoes one more time is that I've had glimpses of the prize—knowing Jesus. Experiencing the prize motivates me to do the tough training.

—Denise

CONNECTING WITH GOD'S FAMILY 10 min.

In order to support each other in our spiritual growth, we need to build strong connections with each other. One way we do this is by continually sharing pieces of our lives. As we do so, keep in mind that each of us is a work in progress and that God can work in each of our lives. Please share your answer to question 1 below. Try to limit your story to about a minute so we'll have plenty of time for the rest of the study.

1. Think of a season in your life when you felt that you were really growing spiritually. What were some of the ingredients that helped you grow?

2. It's important for every group to agree on a set of shared values. If your group doesn't already have an agreement (sometimes called a covenant), turn to page 69. Even if you've been together for some time and your values are clear, the Purpose-Driven Group Agreement can help your group achieve greater health and balance. We recommend that you especially consider rotating group leadership, setting up spiritual partners, and introducing purpose teams into the group. Simply go over the values and expectations listed in the agreement to be sure everyone in the group understands and accepts them. Make any necessary decisions about such issues as refreshments and child care.

GROWING TO BE LIKE CHRIST — 20–30 min.

The Bible describes the *goal* of our lives in various ways: to be transformed into Christ's likeness (2 Corinthians 3:18) or to become complete in Christ (Colossians 1:28).

If that's the goal, what's the *process* by which we get there? The writer to the Hebrews compares the Christian life to a race:

> *Therefore, since we are surrounded by such a great cloud of witnesses, let us throw off everything that hinders and the sin that so easily entangles, and let us run with perseverance the race marked out for us. [2]Let us fix our eyes on Jesus, the author and perfecter of our faith, who for the joy set before him endured the cross, scorning its shame, and sat down at the right hand of the throne of God. [3]Consider him who endured such opposition from sinful men, so that you will not grow weary and lose heart.*
>
> —Hebrews 12:1–3

3. In this passage, what qualities do a race and the Christian life have in common?

4. Salvation is a free gift from God through Jesus Christ. You don't have to earn it; you just believe. Yet a race involves effort. How do you fit together these two truths—salvation as a gift and the Christian life as a race?

5. Greek athletes stripped down to nothing for a race so that nothing would hinder them as they ran. (Luckily, today we have spandex!) So when verse 1 says, "throw off everything," it means *everything* that could potentially hinder you. What are some of the sins that can entangle you and keep you from running the race of Christ well?

6. Even things that aren't sins can be hindrances in your race. Money, career goals, time commitments—anything can be a hindrance if you hold it more dearly than Jesus Christ. What is one thing that hinders your spiritual growth?

7. Why is fixing your eyes on Jesus (verse 2) so essential?

8. Jesus focused on "the joy set before him." What joy is set before you when you finish your race? (See, for example, Hebrews 12:22–24; Philippians 3:20–21; Isaiah 25:6–9.)

9. There are many spiritual practices that will help you stay focused and grow deeper in your walk with Jesus. Over the next five weeks we will review more fully each of the aspects below. Quickly pair up with someone (men with men, women with women) you'd enjoy connecting with, and answer the following question: Which one or two aspects listed below would you like to focus on in this season of your walk with Jesus? Why?

- ☐ Prayer
- ☐ Bible study
- ☐ Surrendering to the Holy Spirit
- ☐ Personal time with God
- ☐ Accountability
- ☐ Journaling

We grow in our walk with God when we experience life together with another Christian friend or in a small group. For the next six weeks, would you be willing to connect briefly (in the group, by E-mail, or by telephone) to encourage another person's spiritual growth? Ask this person now (or during the upcoming week) if you can fill this role.

SHARING YOUR LIFE MISSION EVERY DAY — 10 min.

10. We're not meant to run the race alone. It's always more motivating to run with a pack of other runners. We need the support of fellow runners. You probably know someone who is struggling to run the Christian race alone. Pull an open chair into the circle of your group. This chair represents someone you could invite to join your group.

Who could that person be? Think about family members, friends, neighbors, parents of your kids' friends, church members, coworkers, and the persons who share your hobbies. Take a moment now to prayerfully list one or two names, and then share the names with your group.

____________________ NAME

____________________ NAME

Commit to

- making the call this week. Why not?—over 50 percent of those invited to a small group say yes! You may even want to invite him or her to ride with you.
- calling your church office to get the names of new members, and inviting new members who live near you to visit your group.
- serving your group by praying for and welcoming new people to your group.

SURRENDERING YOUR LIFE FOR GOD'S PLEASURE 15–30 min.

You're not running the race alone! You're surrounded by a cloud of witnesses (Hebrews 12:1)—the generations of faithful men and women who have gone before you. You also have fellow group members who want to support you.

11. On page 83 you'll find a list of brief passages for daily devotions—five per week for the six weeks of this study. If you've never spent daily time with God, this is an easy way to begin. Would you consider taking on this habit for the duration of this study? See page 86 for a sample journal page you can use as a guide for your daily devotions.

    If you're already consistent in daily devotions, consider acquiring the habit of Scripture memory. Six memory verses are provided on page 82—one verse per week. Would you consider accepting the challenge to memorize one verse per week and hide God's Word in your heart? We urge you to pair up with another person for encouragement and accountability.

12. In order to allow more prayer time for everyone, quickly gather into small circles of three or four people. Allow everyone to answer this question: "How can we pray for you this week?" Share personal concerns, as well as some specific ways you would like God to help you throw off things that hinder you from running your race.

    Take some time to pray for these requests in your small circles. Anyone who isn't used to praying aloud should feel free to offer prayers in silence. Or, if you're new to prayer and you're feeling brave, try praying just one sentence: "Thank you, God, for. . . ." Be sure to have one person write down your requests and share them later with the group or leaders.

STUDY NOTES

Hebrews 12 encourages believers to endure hardships and keep running the Christian life. Runners would agree that a cheering crowd, the right equipment, and a clear goal help them press through the pain and cross the finish line.

Such a great cloud of witnesses. Competitors in a race often feel motivated by the presence of spectators. The writer here refers not just to spectators but to actual "witnesses" who attest to the validity of our race. In chapter 11, he lists many faithful men and women who lived and died in faith. He wants his readers to imagine generations of past runners cheering them on.

Perseverance. Endurance. The commitment to remain under some kind of pressure rather than try to escape it. In session 6 you'll look at James 1:3 and see that endurance produces proven character. Responding to difficulties with persistent faith, not scrambling to get out from under hardships, is what produces proven character.

The joy set before him. Jesus looked forward to the joy of returning to his Father and the joy of seeing *us* freed and restored to our Father. We endure the race because of the great reward that is ahead of us—the joy of the Father's embrace.

Fix our eyes. To look away from one thing and to concentrate on another. The idea is to look away from all other distractions and look solely at Jesus, the one who invented and perfected the race.

☐ ***For Further Study*** *on the topic of the Christian life as a race, see Philippians 3:12–14; 1 Corinthians 9:24–27; Galatians 5:7; Acts 20:24; 2 Timothy 4:6–8.*

☐ ***Weekly Memory Verse***: Matthew 6:33

☐ ***The Purpose-Driven Life Reading Plan:*** Day 22

NOTES

If you're using the DVD along with this curriculum, please use this space to take notes on the teaching for this session.

SESSION 2 THE POWER FOR LIVING

After college I joined the staff of a commercial real-estate firm. I was gearing up for a lifetime adventure. One problem: Although I had learned the fundamentals of real estate from my father, I knew nothing of the daily life of a real-estate agent. Thankfully, I wasn't thrown to the lions. Two seasoned partners took me under their wings and mentored me. Their instructions were clear: "Whatever *we* do, *you* do. Follow us. Do exactly what we say, and you will become successful. Learn from us. We'll lead the way." I was willing to set aside my preconceived ideas about how to be a successful real-estate agent and trust these men with my career.

I believe that this discipline taught me a lot about my walk with the Lord. God doesn't expect me to go it alone. Nor does he expect me to find my own way and muster up enough inner strength to implement real and lasting change in my life. He gave me the Holy Spirit. He guides, leads, and empowers me to live the Christian life. I have to be willing to yield control to God and let him lead.

By the way, in my first year as a realtor I was rookie of the year. Following the partners' lead paid off!

—Todd

CONNECTING WITH GOD'S FAMILY 10 min.

The image of running a race can give us the impression that following Jesus is all up to us. Not true! If you wanted to become an Olympic athlete, God would probably have to remake your body. Similarly, if you want to become complete in Jesus Christ, you'll have to let the Holy Spirit do some serious work in your life. You can't do it alone. Galatians 3:3 says we're foolish to try to attain our goals by human effort. We have to choose daily to depend on the Holy Spirit.

1. Have you ever been aware of the Holy Spirit strengthening you to do something beyond what you could do in your own power? If so, briefly describe your experience. If not, share one question you have about the Holy Spirit.

GROWING TO BE LIKE CHRIST 20–30 min.

The Bible uses metaphors to help us understand who the Holy Spirit is and how he works. He is like wind blowing among us, acting powerfully, even though he is unseen (John 3:8). He is like fire in his power and brilliance (Acts 2:1–4). He gushes up from within a believer like a spring of water (John 7:37–39), giving life to the individual and to those around. He is pure and sacred, making us like holy temples when he dwells within us (1 Corinthians 3:16). Wind, water, fire—these are images of what is most powerful, uncontrollable, and beautiful.

When we put our faith in Jesus, the Holy Spirit takes up residence within us. He promises to change our character, produce fruit in our lives, and give us new strength when we rely on him.

It's awesome to think about God living within us. But if we're honest, we'll admit that we struggle between the ideal and the real in this area. Relying on God's power rather than on our own resources can seem vague. Exactly how do we do it?

Here are two steps you can take. *First*, you can adopt a habit of looking for and following the Holy Spirit's lead.

> *But I say, walk by the Spirit, and you will not carry out the desire of the flesh. [17]For the flesh sets its desire against the Spirit, and the Spirit against the flesh; for these are in opposition to one another, so that you may not do the things that you please. [18]But if you are led by the Spirit, you are not under the Law. [19]Now the deeds of the flesh are evident, which are: immorality, impurity, sensuality, [20]idolatry, sorcery, enmities, strife, jealousy, outbursts of anger, disputes, dissentions, factions,*

[21]*envying, drunkenness, carousing, and things like these, of which I forewarn you, just as I have forewarned you, that those who practice such things will not inherit the kingdom of God.* [22]*But the fruit of the Spirit is love, joy, peace, patience, kindness, goodness, faithfulness,* [23]*gentleness, self-control; against such things there is no law.* [24]*Now those who belong to Christ Jesus have crucified the flesh with its passions and desires.*

[25]*If we live by the Spirit, let us also walk by the Spirit.* [26]*Let us not become boastful, challenging one another, envying one another.*

—Galatians 5:16–26 NASB

2. "The deeds of the flesh" are wrongful acts that come naturally to sinful humans. Look over the list in verses 19–21 above, and see if any one of them describes you.

Sorcery may not be on the list of your personal struggles; maybe your list looks more like the one in the left-hand column below. On your own, with no one else looking on, add to this list two or three fleshly habits that are big problems for you.

Deeds of the Flesh	Fruit of the Spirit
Flirting with married people	
Looking down on certain people	
Envying someone's income or waistline	
Holding a grudge against someone	
Gossiping about someone	
Compulsive overspending	
Using computer, television, food, or exercise to avoid painful issues	
Other:	

3. In the right-hand column above, write two aspects of the Spirit's fruit in which you would most like to grow. For example, "more patience with my kids," "more self-control in my workplace," "more loving actions toward my spouse." Without necessarily revealing what you wrote down, share with the group how it affects you to look at what you wrote.

4. If it's up to you and your own willpower, how easy will it be for you to do less of the things in the left column and more of the ones in the right column? Why is that so?

5. The apostle Paul says that you can do more of the things in the right column and less of the ones in the left if you "walk by the Spirit" (Galatians 5:16, 25). See the definition for "walk by the Spirit" on page 30. On a practical level, what does walking by (yielding to, being led by) the Spirit involve for you this week? Think about how you might yield in the areas you identified in the left and right columns above.

Following the Spirit's lead is one step you can take. A *second* step is to adopt a habit of asking for the Spirit's help.

> *For this reason I kneel before the Father, [15]from whom his whole family in heaven and on earth derives its name. [16]I pray that out of his glorious riches he may strengthen you with power through his Spirit in your inner being, [17]so that Christ may dwell in your hearts through faith. And I pray that you, being rooted*

and established in love, [18]may have power, together with all the saints, to grasp how wide and long and high and deep is the love of Christ, [19]and to know this love that surpasses knowledge—that you may be filled to the measure of all the fullness of God.

—Ephesians 3:14–19

6. According to this passage, what will strengthening from the Spirit do for you?

- Verse 17

- Verse 18

- Verse 19

The Spirit empowers you to know Christ's love. But what does that have to do with resisting the flesh and living with patience and goodness? Think about it: Are you willing to give up your favorite feel-good sin just because you're supposed to? Maybe not. Would you be willing to do it for someone who loves you the way you've always longed to be loved? Someone who loves you enough to die for you? Would you risk life and limb to follow a Commander whom you trust implicitly and who treats you with the respect you've always wanted from a great leader? Really knowing Christ's love will empower you to choose the Spirit over the flesh.

7. On your own, complete this sentence: "I would trust God to lead me in the area of ________________ for a God like this: ____."

8. When you pray for the Spirit's power, it's important to accompany it with a desire to leave behind any known sin and to fulfill God's plan for your life. A prayer for the Spirit's power is a prayer of surrender. You choose to say, "Father, I give you my life. Please fill me now and use me in whatever way you want."

   One form of this prayer of surrender is called "spiritual breathing." As you exhale, you confess any known sin. (First John 1:9 says, "If we confess our sins, he is faithful and just and will forgive us our sins and purify us from all unrighteousness.") As you inhale, you pray to breathe in the Holy Spirit.

   Take a few minutes to get a taste of spiritual breathing. Close your eyes. Inhale slowly while you count to four. Exhale slowly to a count of four. Inhale again, letting yourself relax. And exhale. Keep breathing slowly. As you exhale, offer to God any sin you're becoming aware of in yourself—a time today when you lost patience with someone, an area where you're having trouble trusting God or doing what you know is right. As you inhale, ask the Holy Spirit to strengthen you with power in your inner being. Exhale your self-centeredness and self-reliance. Inhale the Father's forgiveness and Christ's love through the Holy Spirit. Pray in your heart as your group leader prays aloud:

   Father, please forgive us for the wrong things we have done this week. We identify our sin silently to you right now. Forgive us for failing to do the good we should have done. Forgive our lack of attention to you. Please strengthen us with power through your Spirit so that Christ may dwell in our hearts. Root us in your love. Enable us to grasp how wide and long and high and deep it is. Fill us with your Spirit, so that we may do the things you want done in the world. We give you our whole lives. Amen.

DEVELOPING YOUR SHAPE TO SERVE OTHERS 15–20 min.

9. What can God do in your life through the Spirit's power? More than you can imagine! The Purpose-Driven Life Health Assessment on page 74 is a tool to help you identify the state of your heart in various areas. Take a few minutes right now to

rate yourself in the GROWING section of the assessment. You won't have to share your scores with the group.

10. Pair up with your partner from last week or someone in the group with whom you feel comfortable discussing your assessment. We recommend that men partner with men and women with women. Groups of three are also fine. Talk about these three questions:

    - **What's hot?** (In what ways are you doing well?)
    - **What's not?** (In which areas do you need the most growth?)
    - **What's next?** (What is one goal that you think God would like you to work on over the next thirty days? What will you do to reach this goal?)

    Here are examples of possible goals:

    - ☐ At least three days a week I will spend ten minutes a day in God's Word.
    - ☐ At least three days a week I will use a journal to write out my prayers.
    - ☐ I will focus my prayers this month on the issue of growing in faith instead of in fear, asking the Holy Spirit for specific help.
    - ☐ I will set aside a half hour each week to reflect on Psalm 23 in order to plant in my heart the truth that God is shepherding me and therefore I have nothing to fear.
    - ☐ I will check in with ________________ at least once a week to let him or her know how I'm doing at focusing on faith instead of on fear in my current situation.

    Write your goal here:

The person you've paired up with can be your spiritual partner to support you in reaching your goal. In two of the next four group sessions you will briefly check in with your spiritual partner about your personal progress. Use the Spiritual Partners' Check-In Page (page 79) to plot your plans and progress. You can also call or send an E-mail to each other between meetings.

If you've never taken the Purpose-Driven Life Health Assessment, consider rating yourself in the remaining four areas on your own this week.

SURRENDERING YOUR LIFE FOR GOD'S PLEASURE 15–20 min.

11. Stay with your spiritual partner(s) for prayer. Take a few minutes to share any other prayer requests that haven't already surfaced in your discussion. Then pray for each other, especially for the Spirit's power to fulfill the plans you have made. If you're new to group prayer, it's okay to pray silently or to pray by using just one sentence. You might choose a sentence from the prayer you prayed earlier:

Please strengthen us with power through your Spirit so that Christ may dwell in our hearts. Root us in your love. Enable us to grasp how wide and long and high and deep it is. Fill us with your Spirit, so that we may do the things you want done in the world. We give you our whole lives. Amen.

As you leave, remember

- your goal for the next thirty days.
- to keep on with your daily devotions.
- to hide God's Word in your heart through your weekly Scripture memory verse.

STUDY NOTES

Walk by the Spirit. In other words, move through your life in step with, led by, and empowered by the Holy Spirit (Romans 8:9). Romans 8:14 and Galatians 5:18 use a related phrase—"led by the Spirit." The Holy Spirit leads as a guide or mentor. We yield to the Spirit's leading by walking along with him. We humbly acknowledge in prayer and in obedience to the Word that the Spirit knows better than we do. We ask the Spirit for direction and seek for truth to follow (see John 14:26).

Flesh. In this context, not the flesh and bones of our physical bodies, but the fallen aspects of humankind that persist in us even after God has made us spiritually alive in Jesus Christ (Ephesians 2:3–5). Flesh includes instinctive qualities run amok, such as natural impulses for sex or for survival that are distorted into lust or selfishness or greed. It includes all kinds of strategies for keeping our lives under control without God's help. Addictions and compulsions are also fleshly. (See 1 Corinthians 3:1–3 for an explanation of fleshly living.)

The flesh sets its desire against the Spirit. Your flesh has a deep-rooted desire to indulge in whatever sin it deems necessary in order for you to survive and feel good. Each person's flesh tends to become attached to certain sins that seem to "work" for that person. When the Holy Spirit takes up residence in you and tries to lead you away from those sins, a full-scale war breaks out. Letting go of a favorite sin can make you feel as though you're dying; indeed, your flesh *is* dying, and it doesn't like it! But as you yield to the Spirit's control and starve the flesh, you experience the fruit of your labor.

☐ ***For Further Study*** *on the filling and leading of the Holy Spirit, read Luke 11:9–13; Acts 1:8; Ephesians 4:29–32; 5:15–18; 1 John 1:9.*

☐ ***Weekly Memory Verse:*** Ephesians 3:16–17

☐ ***The Purpose-Driven Life Reading Plan:*** Day 23

NOTES

If you're using the DVD along with this curriculum, please use this space to take notes on the teaching for this session.

SESSION 3

PERSONAL TIME WITH GOD

Many years ago, I formed in my mind an image of what it looks like to spend time with God. I picked up this image from a friend whose spiritual life I admired. Dave was gentle with people, always encouraging, yet firm with his convictions. He was the first person you'd go to with a problem or concern. You knew he'd listen to you and offer wise counsel from God's Word. Dave's wife told me that for years he sat in the same leather chair in their living room each morning before work to read his Bible and talk to God. He left his Bible on the table by that particular chair each night, so it would be ready for him the next morning. So, naturally, the day we were invited to their house for dinner, I wanted to see that chair. As I walked into his house, there it was in the living room, just as I had imagined it.

I have since found a similar place for myself. When I see that place, it's a great reminder each morning to pause and spend some time with God. Although I struggle to stay consistent, I have found that my time with the Lord is producing the change of character and perspective I long for in my life.

—Todd

CONNECTING WITH GOD'S FAMILY — 10 min.

For many of us, the first barrier to time alone with God is just getting time alone! In a culture that values productivity and has high expectations about what we should accomplish each day, we may find it hard to justify taking time to do something that is neither productive nor entertaining according to the world's standards.

1. In a typical week, approximately how much time do you spend alone? Approximately how much time do you spend alone with God?

GROWING TO BE LIKE CHRIST

30–40 min.

God longs to cultivate a deep relationship with each of us. He jealously seeks those who will seek him (Jeremiah 29:13). Even though we may believe this and may even have experienced it, most of us have difficulty sustaining a regular time with God. Creating a time when we simply sit at the feet of Jesus and enjoy his presence has been a common struggle since the first century. Read the story of Mary and Martha, and see whether you can identify:

> *As Jesus and his disciples were on their way, he came to a village where a woman named Martha opened her home to him. [39]She had a sister called Mary, who sat at the Lord's feet listening to what he said. [40]But Martha was distracted by all the preparations that had to be made. She came to him and asked, "Lord, don't you care that my sister has left me to do the work by myself? Tell her to help me!" [41]"Martha, Martha," the Lord answered, "you are worried and upset about many things, [42]but only one thing is needed. Mary has chosen what is better, and it will not be taken away from her."*
>
> —Luke 10:38–42

2. What is Jesus trying to communicate to Martha in this story?

3. Imagine that you're Martha. You have at least thirteen houseguests for dinner. How would you defend your point of view?

4. Why does Jesus think Mary has chosen what is better?

5. What are some of the things that help or motivate you to set aside time to be alone with God?

6. What is one feature about your life that interferes with time alone with God?

7. *(Optional)* What are the advantages of cultivating personal time with God and his Word? Have different group members each look up one of the following Bible passages and read it aloud:

   - Psalm 19:7–8
   - Psalm 62:1–2
   - Psalm 63:1–3
   - Joshua 1:8
   - 1 Peter 2:2

   Which one of these reasons encourages you the most?

8. Take the next ten or fifteen minutes to experience personal time with God. Group members can scatter to separate rooms or just sit quietly in the same room.

   Focus your full attention on the Lord. Look up Matthew 6:25–34 in your Bible and read it prayerfully. After reading these ten verses, briefly respond to these questions, either here or in your journal (these two questions can be used to reflect on any Bible passage):

- Who are you, Lord?

  You are a God who . . .

- What do you want me to do?

  You want me to . . .

9. After ten minutes of spending time with God, come back together and share how God spoke to you.

DEVELOPING YOUR SHAPE TO SERVE OTHERS 10 min.

10. Healthy small groups seek to balance all five purposes of the church deep within the heart of every member (see pages 11–14). You should get every member's gifts in the game, because every member is a minister and you ultimately want to share ownership with the entire group. Take a moment to identify which group members would be gifted in which areas. (It's fine to let two people share a role.) Write the names of the people in the space to the left of each purpose. Also circle one or two areas you'd be open to helping out with.

_______ CONNECTING: Plan a social event for the group, *and/or* call unconnected or absent members each week to see how they're doing.

_______ **GROWING:** Encourage personal devotions through group discussions and spiritual (accountability) partners, *and/or* facilitate a three- or four-person discussion during your Bible study next week.

_______ **DEVELOPING:** Ensure that every member finds a group role or responsibility, *and/or* coordinate a group service project in your church or community.

_______ **SHARING:** Collect names of unchurched friends for whom the group could pray and share updates, *and/or* help launch a six-week starter group with other friends or unconnected people.

_______ **SURRENDERING:** Coordinate the group's prayer and praise list (a list of prayer requests and answers to prayer), *and/or* lead the group in a brief worship time, using a CD, video, or instrument.

SURRENDERING YOUR LIFE FOR GOD'S PLEASURE 10–30 min.

For [the Lord] satisfieth the longing soul, and filleth the hungry soul with goodness.

—Psalm 107:9 KJV

11. Sit next to your spiritual partner(s) or pair up with another member. Together do one or more of the following:

    - Share what you learned from your devotional time this week.
    - Recite your memory verse.
    - Tell how you're doing with the goal you set for yourself.

12. Team up with another pair of spiritual partners to form a prayer circle. Share a brief prayer request. Have one person write down the requests. Then pray for each other, especially to overcome obstacles that stand in the way of making time to be with God. If you're new to praying aloud, try praying one sentence: "Lord, please ______________________." If you prefer to pray silently, you can simply say "amen" to let the group know you're finished.

STUDY NOTES

Martha . . . Mary. These sisters were Jesus' close friends. Their brother was Lazarus, whom Jesus later raised from the dead (John 11:43). See also John 11:1–6; 12:1–8; Matthew 27:61. We find Martha serving and Mary sitting at the Lord's feet on other occasions.

Sat at Jesus' feet. This was the posture of Jewish scholars while listening to a rabbi's teaching. It was highly unusual for a first-century teacher to accept a woman as a disciple.

Listening. The Greek verb here *(akouō)* means not only to listen but also to understand. It takes a special kind of listening to understand what is being said. It requires patience, attentiveness, and prayerful thought.

What he said. Literally, "his word." The Greek word here *(logon)* refers to the actual words of God. Jesus spoke God's words to the disciples. When we spend time reading the Bible, we are listening to Jesus' words, much as Mary did.

Distracted . . . worried . . . upset. The burden of Martha's duties had drawn away her attention. Our English word *worry* comes from the old German *wurgen*, which means "to strangle or to choke." Worry and distractions choke our spiritual lives to death!

☐ ***For Further Study*** *on the idea of spending time alone with God, see Matthew 14:23; Mark 6:31; Isaiah 55:1–3; 2 Timothy 3:16–17.*

☐ ***Weekly Memory Verse***: Luke 10:41–42

☐ ***The Purpose-Driven Life Reading Plan:*** Day 24

Tips for a Fruitful Personal Time with God

1. Set a definite time—a time when you will be most alert.
2. Choose a quiet place—a place where you won't be disturbed.
3. Start out with just ten or fifteen minutes.
4. Include Bible reading, prayer, and confession of any sin you're aware of.
5. Be habitual about it; it takes about six weeks to develop a new habit.
6. Determine ahead of time what you are going to do. (The format of asking "Who are you, Lord?" and "What do you want me to do?" is one option.)
7. Be creative; consider varying the things you do during your quiet time (Bible reading, listening to a worship CD, journaling your praise to God, meditating on a single verse or passage of Scripture).
8. Write down in a journal what you are learning about God and what you believe he wants you to do (submit to correction, respond in a specific act of obedience, offer him praise, accept his forgiveness, bow before him in repentance).

NOTES

If you're using the DVD along with this curriculum, please use this space to take notes on the teaching for this session.

SESSION 4

ENTERING GOD'S PRESENCE

About five years ago I went with a friend to a retreat in Wisconsin. The retreat leader talked about the endless love and faithfulness of God, no matter what we do or what circumstances we face. It was just the simple message of "Jesus loves me, this I know," but it hit home for me.

After one particular session, I went to my room and got down on my knees. I wanted to bring before God all that was going on in my life. My window faced a beautiful lake, and I was gazing out as I prayed, imagining God on the shoreline across the lake. My friend walked in and asked what I was doing. I told her, and she said, "Oh, it's so interesting that, when you pray, you picture God so far away. When I pray, I envision him right beside me. Or I'm on his lap, and he's gently embracing me in the warmth of his loving arms."

God used that particular afternoon to forever change my view of him. He is not a loving-yet-distant heavenly Father. He is intimate. He knows my name and my thoughts, my joys and my challenges. He simply loves me in the midst of my weaknesses, and he desires a growing friendship with me. He is here right now.

—Dee

CONNECTING WITH GOD'S FAMILY — 10 min.

Prayer can pose a dilemma. It promises closeness with God and awareness of his love for us. It helps us obtain freedom from guilt and shame and feel acceptance, hope, and peace. It's a doorway to wisdom—and sometimes even to miracles. But for many of us, prayer feels like an area of failure. We may feel we're just not "good" at prayer. We may begin to question how spiritual we really are if we have so much trouble praying.

1. Complete the following two sentences:

   - One good thing about my prayer life recently is ________

     ____

• One challenge I have in praying is ____________________

____

GROWING TO BE LIKE CHRIST 40 min.

One day Jesus' disciples asked him, "Lord, teach us to pray" (Luke 11:1). Evidently it wasn't so easy for them either! Jesus taught them, "This, then, is how you should pray" (Matthew 6:9). He gave them an outline for prayer, which we call the Lord's Prayer. Many Christians today pray the Lord's Prayer word for word, but it's also useful as an outline for spontaneous prayer.

> *And when you pray, do not be like the hypocrites, for they love to pray standing in the synagogues and on the street corners to be seen by men. I tell you the truth, they have received their reward in full. [6]But when you pray, go into your room, close the door and pray to your Father, who is unseen. Then your Father, who sees what is done in secret, will reward you. [7]And when you pray, do not keep on babbling like pagans, for they think they will be heard because of their many words. [8]Do not be like them, for your Father knows what you need before you ask him.*
>
> *[9]This, then, is how you should pray:*
>
> *"Our Father in heaven,*
> *hallowed be your name,*
> *[10]your kingdom come,*
> *your will be done*
> *on earth as it is in heaven.*
> *[11]Give us today our daily bread.*
> *[12]Forgive us our debts,*
> *as we also have forgiven our debtors.*
> *[13]And lead us not into temptation,*
> *but deliver us from the evil one."*
>
> —Matthew 6:5–13

In order to give everyone in the group a chance to talk in this Bible study, consider breaking into discussion circles of three or four people if your group is larger than seven. In each small circle, the person whose birthday is closest to today will guide the discussion.

2. What tips for an authentic prayer life do you get from verses 5–8?

3. In his prayer outline, Jesus begins with this theme: **"Our Father in heaven, hallowed be your name."** (See page 48 for the meaning of *heaven* and *hallowed.*) Jesus asks us to

- address prayer to someone we know as "Father"—one who is as near to us as the air (atmosphere, heaven) we breathe.
- begin by focusing on our Father's grand qualities and capabilities.

How do you feel about addressing God as "my Father who is right here with me"?

4. Why might it be helpful to start your prayer by focusing on your Father's greatness?

5. Jesus goes on, **"Your kingdom come, your will be done on earth as it is in heaven."** This petition establishes our willingness to surrender our plans to God and to participate in doing our Father's will. Many Christians understand this concept but struggle to put it into practice consistently.

Give an example of something that you know is God's will for you to do this week. (For example, God wants you to treat your annoying coworker with respect.)

6. How might you turn your answer to question 5 into a prayer, surrendering yourself to do God's will in this specific area?

7. **"Give us today our daily bread."** This request expresses our dependence on God to provide for our every need. Each time we eat, drink, earn money, or buy something, we can recall that God is the one who provides these things. Our Father wants to stay connected with us on a *daily* basis.

   Share with the group one of your daily needs right now. Pause to pray for each member as the need is shared. (The leader can pray one or two sentences, or someone else in the group can volunteer to pray a sentence or two for the person who has shared.)

8. **"Forgive us our debts [sins]"** expresses our need to keep our communication clean and clear with our Father. Has disobedience ever interfered with your connection to God? If so, what happened when you sought forgiveness?

9. **"And lead us not into temptation, but deliver us from the evil one."** This request expresses our need for protection from the real forces of the evil one. Again, many Christians understand this truth but don't live with an active awareness of it.

   Are you experiencing any trial or hardship that tempts you to disobey or to become discouraged? If so, share briefly with the group the way in which you're being tempted.

10. To become more comfortable talking with our Father, it can be helpful to write out our prayers. Take five or ten minutes on your own to write a prayer. You can use the following outline if you like:

    Dear Father who . . . (Write something about God that you marvel at. This is called praise, worship, honor, adoration.)

    I so much want to see that your will is done in the area of . . .

    Please give me and those I love . . . (Write things you'd like God to do for you or for others. This is called supplication, intercession, or just plain asking for help!)

Forgive me for . . . (Write down any items you need to clear up with God. This is called confession.)

I forgive . . . (Any grudges to let go of?)

Please protect me or others from . . .

Thank you, Father!

DEVELOPING YOUR SHAPE TO SERVE OTHERS 10 min.

Today you did your Bible study in small circles of three or four people. When you do this, others besides your official leader have the opportunity to develop skills in leading a discussion. There might be someone in your group with leadership gifts waiting to be developed.

Consider giving one or more group members the chance to be a facilitator for a meeting. Healthy groups rotate their leadership each week. No one person has to carry all the responsibility. What's more, it helps develop everyone's gifts in a safe environment, and, best of all, you learn different things through the eyes of different people with different styles. You can use the Small Group Calendar (page 71) to help manage your rotating schedule.

11. If your leader were to be absent, who is the person in your group you would choose as your second leader? Who has the heart of a shepherd and enough skill to guide a discussion? Let everyone select the person he or she would choose and briefly share the reason.

    Are you surprised? Most groups find remarkable agreement about the person among them who has the heart and potential for small group leadership. Often groups choose someone who would never volunteer but who has the heart of a shepherd. Be sure to ask whether the person selected would be willing to colead the group for the duration of the study.

SURRENDERING YOUR LIFE FOR GOD'S PLEASURE 10–20 min.

12. Consider sharing Communion together next week. It's a wonderful way to celebrate your heavenly Father. If you decide to share Communion, ask the group who would be a good person or team to lead it? Who will bring the elements?

    Instructions for sharing Communion in a small group are on page 80.

    You've already shared some prayer requests and prayed together, but you can close now in prayer if you choose. You might encourage everyone to stand, hold hands, and sing a simple closing song ("Praise God from Whom All Blessings Flow," "Jesus Loves Me," "I Love You, Lord," and the like).

STUDY NOTES

Hypocrites. The Greek word literally means "actors." In Greek theaters (there was one in Galilee near the place where Jesus lived) actors performed while wearing masks. Hypocrites are like actors in that they treat life—even the act of prayer—as a theatrical performance and often hide their true identities behind masks.

Heaven. In the ancient world, the Greek word for heaven *(ouranos)* referred to the atmosphere, the sky, the realms beyond the sky, and the spiritual realm of God. The "first heaven" was the atmosphere or air that surrounds humans on earth. Beyond that was the rest of "the heavens." God occupies all of this space—including the farthest galaxy and the atmosphere you are breathing. In the Old Testament, God frequently speaks "from heaven" (Genesis 21:17–19; 22:11, 15), which often appears to mean "out of the air close by" not "from somewhere far away in the sky." Thus, "Father in heaven" means "Father who is right here next to me, even though I can't see you," as well as, "Father who is beyond the universe."

Hallowed be your name. *Hallowed* means "holy"—that which is perfect, free from the contamination of sin. God alone is holy and is worthy of our praise because of his holiness.

Your kingdom come, your will be done. The kingdom of God is the realm where all who exist in it live by the will of God. Jesus is the King, so when he came to earth, the kingdom had arrived. Anyone who received Jesus would enter into a new realm—God's kingdom—even while they lived on this earth. Our prayer is to live in that realm and to fulfill God's will for our lives.

Lead us not into temptation. This petition has often been confusing. Does God tempt us? No. (See James 1:13–18.) Jesus wants us to pray that God will keep us from temptation. Matthew Henry wrote, "Lord, do not let Satan loose upon us; chain up that roaring lion, for he is subtle and spiteful; Lord, do not leave us to ourselves (Psalm 19:13), for we are very weak; Lord, do not lay stumbling-blocks and snares before us, nor put us into circumstances that may be an occasion of falling."*

**Matthew Henry's Commentary on the Whole Bible: New Modern Edition*, Electronic Database (Peabody, Mass.: Hendrickson, 1991).

☐ **For Further Study** *on the topic of prayer, read Philippians 4:6–7; Mark 1:35; 2 Chronicles 7:14; 1 Thessalonians 5:17; Jude 20.*

☐ **Weekly Memory Verse**: *Psalm 46:10*

☐ ***The Purpose-Driven Life* Reading Plan:** Day 25

NOTES

If you're using the DVD along with this curriculum, please use this space to take notes on the teaching for this session.

SESSION 5

A TASTE FOR GOD'S WORD

There was a time in my life when consistent Bible reading paid off. I had been molested as a child, and I carried into adulthood a feeling that I was somehow dirty. I felt myself unworthy of a good man. Eventually I made my way into counseling, but a year of talking through my childhood didn't lift that sense of dirtiness.

During that time I was reading my Bible each day. I read through the Gospels and continually identified with the lepers and outcasts. I wished that Jesus would touch me the way he touched the leper and made him clean. Eventually I reached the middle of the book of Acts. In Acts 10:9–23 I read about a vision God gave Peter to convince him that God had opened the door of faith to the disreputable Gentiles. Three times in the vision a voice ordered Peter, "Do not call anything impure that God has made clean."

I stared at the verse. I felt as though God was giving me an order. I started to cry. I realized that Jesus had probably touched me months or even years ago—the way he touched the leper—but I hadn't believed him.

I knew that if my counselor had simply quoted the verse to me, I might not have heard it in my heart. God had been able to get through to me because I had been reading the New Testament consistently. God had used the stories from the Gospels, and I came to Acts with a prepared heart.

I memorized the verse from Acts. After that, whenever the old feelings of dirtiness began to creep back in, I quoted the verse to myself. On my wedding day, God's words were there for me.

—Karen

CONNECTING WITH GOD'S FAMILY

10 min.

Bible study is easier for some people than for others. Some of us are naturally more inclined toward the study of books, especially books written thousands of years ago. Also, some of us were raised in homes in which the Bible was read and used often, while others were raised in homes where the Bible was unknown. For these reasons and more, God understands that we are all at different places in our growth as students of the Word.

1. What place did the Bible have in your home, if any, when you were growing up?

2. What place did the Bible have in your life five years ago?

GROWING TO BE LIKE CHRIST 30–40 min.

Personal Bible study is one of the most enriching and rewarding experiences in the Christian life. It's not easy, but it is rewarding. The Scriptures tell us that if we spend time in personal study, we are blessed, approved by God, stable, successful, and prosperous (Psalm 1). If we want these qualities in our lives, how do we obtain them? By deciding to spend time each week studying God's Word for ourselves. Even though our fears and excuses may be understandable, we need to lay them aside and take a first step today.

Spend the next fifteen minutes doing the following Bible study on your own. Then share with the group what you discovered. You're going to use a method called *Observation-Interpretation-Application*.

Before you dig into your study, knowing a little background is usually helpful. That's why we've provided the study notes on pages 57–58.

3. **Observation.** Imagine that you're a detective—like Sherlock Holmes. Your first step is to observe as many details as you possibly can: the footprint, the cigar stub, the scarlet thread on the carpet. When observing a Bible passage, you ask yourself questions—who? what? when? where? how? why? Read the following passage several times, each time asking the who, what, when, where, how, why questions. Write down your answers. A "who" question is done for you as an example.

   Do nothing out of selfish ambition or vain conceit, but in humility consider others better than yourselves. [4]Each of you should look not only to your own interests, but also to the interests of others.

[5]*Your attitude should be the same as that of Christ Jesus:*

[6]*Who, being in very nature God,*
did not consider equality with God something to be grasped,
[7]*but made himself nothing,*
taking the very nature of a servant,
being made in human likeness.
[8]*And being found in appearance as a man,*
he humbled himself
and became obedient to death—even death on a cross!
[9]*Therefore God exalted him to the highest place*
and gave him the name that is above every name,
[10]*that at the name of Jesus every knee should bow,*
in heaven and on earth and under the earth,
[11]*and every tongue confess that Jesus Christ is Lord,*
to the glory of God the Father.

—Philippians 2:3–11

Who is involved here?

- *"Yourselves, you, your" (verses 3–5)—this refers to the Philippians*
- *Paul (not mentioned, but he's the writer of this letter)*
- *"Christ Jesus" (verses 5, 11)*
- *"God the Father" (verse 11)*

What does Paul say about each of these persons?

When?

Where?

How do people relate or respond to each other?

Why?

4. **Interpretation.** Now that you've gathered the facts, it's time to ask, "What does it all mean?" Meaning comes from the connections between the facts. Here are some connections you can look for in a passage:

   - What *comparisons* between things do you notice in this passage? (Look for such words as "the same as," "so also," and "like.")

   - What *contrasts* between things do you notice? (Look for such words as "but," "yet," and "however.")

*"[Jesus] did not consider equality with God something to be grasped, **but** made himself nothing" (verses 6–7, emphasis added): These words contrast what Jesus could have done with what he chose to do.*

- What examples do you see of *one thing causing another*? (Look for such words as "therefore," "consequently," and "so.")

- What *key words* make an impression on you?

- Now that you've seen some connections, how would you summarize the *main point* the writer is trying to make?

5. **Application.** The final question is always, "So what?" What are you going to do, based on what you've learned from this passage? (Be specific and realistic.)

6. After fifteen minutes, stop and gather as a group. It's okay if you've spent the whole time doing observations! Take another few moments to debrief.

   - What did you observe?
   - What connections and main point did you discover?
   - What will you do in response?
   - What did you learn about Bible study?
   - What lingering questions do you have about the passage or the process?

   If you're not already doing daily devotions, consider using this Bible study method for five days this week, using the devotional verses below:

   ☐ Psalm 1:1–3
   ☐ Isaiah 55:1–3
   ☐ 2 Timothy 3:16–17
   ☐ Psalm 19:7–11
   ☐ Hebrews 4:12–13

SHARING YOUR LIFE MISSION EVERY DAY 10 min.

7. Jesus became a servant in order to win salvation for you. Paul asked the Philippians to adopt Jesus' attitude of servanthood in their relationships. Brainstorm as a group several ideas for reaching out and serving in your community. Where could you bring a cup of cold water in Jesus' name? Then decide which group member could best coordinate this activity.

SURRENDERING YOUR LIFE FOR GOD'S PLEASURE 10–30 min.

8. Sit next to your spiritual partner(s). Together do one or more of the following:

   - Share what you learned from your devotional time this week.

- Recite your memory verse.
- Tell how you're doing with the goal you set for yourself.

9. To celebrate this part of your journey together, you may want to share Communion. By honoring Jesus and his death on the cross, Communion is a valuable way to remember what the Lord has done for you. It's a chance to reflect on the humility the Son of God took on in order to extend his unconditional love to you. It's an opportunity to thank him for all that he's done.

   Instructions for sharing Communion in a small group are on page 80.

10. How can the group pray for you this week? Share requests and then close in prayer.

STUDY NOTES

It's helpful to know a little about the book you're studying before diving into a passage. Any good study Bible will give you some basic background about the book. Today's passage is from a letter the apostle Paul wrote to believers in Philippi. Paul is writing from jail—he has been arrested for preaching about Jesus Christ. From this unlikely setting, Paul writes about joy. One secret to joy, he explains in chapter 2, is through serving others.

Bible passages contain words and phrases that are rich with meaning. If you're interested in mining the depth of a passage, reference books can enlighten you about words like these:

Humility. Lowliness of mind. Humility is how we think, not just how we speak or act. It's the attitude that acknowledges that we are insufficient in ourselves and therefore completely dependent on God's power. It's not an expression of self-contempt but rather a willingness to be realistic about our weakness and dependence. Recognizing that we're not the stars of the show, we become willing and eager to serve others.

Consider. To come to a judgment or position through careful evaluation of the facts. We consider others' needs to be more important than our own by taking the time to discern and evaluate what someone else's needs are.

Made himself nothing. This refers to the *kenosis*, or emptying, of Jesus Christ. Jesus did not lose his deity when he became a man, but he voluntarily chose not to use some aspects of his deity while on earth. It's hard to imagine what it was like for someone with divine greatness to empty himself of that greatness. He was in only one place at a time. He felt pain. He worked and served. He needed food and drink and rest. He needed time away from work in order to pray. He couldn't serve others twenty-four hours a day. The Unlimited One took on limits. He humbly considered others' needs to be more important than his own. He took on the normal needs of a human being. If we are ever tempted to think we can do it all, Jesus' example corrects us. Likewise, if we are ever tempted to think that we are here to be served rather than to spend ourselves in service, Jesus' example again corrects us.

Another way to deepen your study of a passage is to look at *cross references*. These are other Scripture passages that shed light on the one you're studying. Your study Bible usually has a system for directing you to cross references.

☐ ***For Further Study:*** *The following are a few cross references especially related to today's passage: Matthew 11:29; 26:39; Romans 12:16; 2 Corinthians 8:9; Titus 3:1–2; 1 Peter 5:5–7; Numbers 12:3.*

You might also want to study the life of an Old Testament king—King Uzziah—in 2 Chronicles 26:1–21. Pride led to his downfall. Pride—the belief that one is the center of one's universe—is the opposite of humility.

☐ **Weekly Memory Verse**: *2 Timothy 2:15*

☐ ***The Purpose-Driven Life Reading Plan:*** Days 26 and 27

NOTES

If you're using the DVD along with this curriculum, please use this space to take notes on the teaching for this session.

SESSION 6

THE UNLIKELY ROUTE TO JOY

When Dee became pregnant with our third child, I had a perfect Jack-and-Jill picture of our future as a family. I was going to be a hard-driving pastor, while Dee would be raising our children to become the envy of parents everywhere. Then we learned that Dee was carrying triplets. That was the first shock, but I just didn't get it at the time.

Our three girls were born two months before the due date; it was a horrendous delivery that left Dee physically spent and two of our precious babies with cerebral palsy. Suddenly I was drowning in a whirlpool of diapers, feedings, sleepless nights, and nagging questions. What happened to my perfect family? At least one, and possibly two, of my daughters would never walk! This was not my picture of "the abundant life."

I wrestled with God until grief and exhaustion took me to a place I had never been before. God used this dark time to build in me qualities I could not have gained otherwise—constant involvement with my family, Spirit-led endurance, and a dynamic hope that was based on something more substantial than my own brains and energy. I clung to James 1:2–8 and other Bible passages like a drowning man clings to a log, and they carried me through. I wouldn't wish on any parent the pain I've faced, but today I wouldn't trade it for anything.

—Brett

CONNECTING WITH GOD'S FAMILY 10 min.

Because this is the last session in this study guide, it's a good time to celebrate what this group has meant to you.

1. Looking back over your time with the group, how would you complete these sentences:

   - The high point in this study for me up to now has been
     - ☐ praying together.
     - ☐ studying Scripture.
     - ☐ experiencing personal time with God.

- ☐ encouraging each other in our journey.
- ☐ belonging to an authentic community of love and honesty.
- ☐ sharing stories and thoughts.
- ☐ Other: ______________________________

- One of the most significant things I learned was ________
______________________________.

- The thing I appreciate most about the group is (you may want to include your gratitude for what specific members contributed, as well as your appreciation for your leaders)
____
______________________________.

GROWING TO BE LIKE CHRIST — 30–40 min.

Bible study, prayer, and other spiritual practices are tools with which the Holy Spirit cultivates the soil of our lives so that we can bear fruit. But the soil would remain barren if the farmer never dug it up. Fortunately (although it rarely appears so at the time), thunderstorms of hardship roll in, softening the soil with rain so that the Spirit can dig and plant. Sometimes the storms feel like hurricanes, but without them we would not bear fruit. For this reason, James gives us the astonishing advice to *rejoice* when we see the dark clouds gather:

> *Consider it pure joy, my brothers, whenever you face trials of many kinds, [3]because you know that the testing of your faith develops perseverance. [4]Perseverance must finish its work so that you may be mature and complete, not lacking anything. [5]If any of you lacks wisdom, he should ask God, who gives generously to all without finding fault, and it will be given to him. [6]But when he asks, he must believe and not doubt, because he who doubts is like a wave of the sea, blown and tossed by the wind. [7]That man should not think he will receive anything from the Lord; [8]he is a double-minded man, unstable in all he does.*
>
> —James 1:2–8

2. According to James, what do trials accomplish?

3. Read the definition of perseverance on page 65. Why do you suppose James thinks perseverance is so valuable?

4. Think of a trial you have faced. How easy was it at the time for you to "consider it pure joy"?

As you look back on this trial, can you see any ways in which it built perseverance, faith, or maturity in you? If so, explain.

5. Some trials are so awful that it seems outrageous to embrace them as character building. But the fact that God uses terrible events to accomplish good does not mean that he engineers such tragedies simply to help survivors grow. Evil and suffering remain mysteries about which we must not speak glibly. But knowing that God *does* bring good out of terrible events can give us hope.

Have you faced any trials that seem too awful to embrace with joy? If so (and if you are willing), share your thoughts with the group.

6. Trials don't produce perseverance automatically. They can produce bitterness if we so choose. What does James encourage us to do when we face a trial so that the experience will be fruitful (verses 5–8)?

7. For what current trial in your life do you need wisdom in order to respond well?

Gather in pairs or in circles of three or four people to pray for wisdom in these areas.

SHARING YOUR LIFE MISSION EVERY DAY 10 min.

8. *(Optional)* What's next for you personally in your spiritual journey? Here are some possibilities:

☐ I'm going to continue in this group.
☐ I'm willing to take on a new role in this group.
☐ I'm interested in going on to the next study in the DOING LIFE TOGETHER series.
☐ I'm going to take on a new goal for spiritual growth. My goal will be:

____

☐ Other:

9. What's next for your group? Turn to the Purpose-Driven Group Agreement on page 69. Do you want to agree to continue meeting together? If so, do you want to change anything in this agreement (times, dates, shared values, and so on)? Are there any things you'd like the group to do better as it moves forward? Take notes on this discussion.

SURRENDERING YOUR LIFE FOR GOD'S PLEASURE 10–30 min.

10. You prayed for each other during your Bible study, so you may not need to share requests again. Conclude by thanking God for each person in your group and for what God is doing in each person's life. Also pray about what your group will do next, now that you've completed this study.

STUDY NOTES

Whenever. It's not "if" we encounter trials; it's "when." We all face them. Nobody is exempt. We need to expect them without becoming cynical or paranoid.

Trials. The Greek word *peirasmois* includes both trials (painful events) as well as temptations to sin. In this context James probably has trials in mind, because in 1:13 he will take up the issue of temptations.

Of many kinds. Multicolored, various. Trials come in all shapes and sizes. Yours may not be the same as another person's trial. Be careful not to either minimize or overinflate your struggle.

Perseverance. Endurance, the ability to make it over the long haul, the commitment to remain under a trial rather than to try to squirm our way out of it. We often desire to escape a trial, but perseverance enables us to remain under it so that God can form our character. We must hang in there and allow the process of endurance to make us the persons we were created to be.

Mature. Or "perfect" (NASB). The Greek word *teleios* refers to something that has reached its full capacity. A full-grown tree is *teleios*. It has realized the purpose for which it was designed. We become *teleios* by enduring trials. We don't become perfect in the sense of sinless, but we see changes in character, priorities, attitudes, feelings, and behavior.

Wisdom. Insight into what's real, how things work, what's important in life, and how to live well. We can either try to make sense of trials on our own and create strategies for dealing with them, or we can ask God to guide us. God may not answer all of our "why" questions, but he will give us valuable insight into what's important and into how we can live well in the midst of trials.

☐ ***For Further Study*** *on this topic, read 1 Peter 4:12–13; Philippians 1:29; Romans 8:17; 2 Corinthians 1:5.*

☐ ***Weekly Memory Verse****: James 1:2–3*

☐ ***The Purpose-Driven Life Reading Plan:*** Day 28

NOTES

If you're using the DVD along with this curriculum, please use this space to take notes on the teaching for this session.

FREQUENTLY ASKED QUESTIONS

Who may attend the group?

Anybody you feel would benefit from it. As you begin, we encourage each attender to invite at least one other friend to join. A good time to join is in the first or second week of a new study. Share the names of your friends with the group members so that they can be praying for you.

How long will this group meet?

It's totally up to the group—once you come to the end of this six-week study. Most groups meet weekly for at least the first six weeks, but every other week can work as well. At the end of this study, each group member may decide if he or she wants to continue on for another six-week study. We encourage you to consider using the next study in this series. The series is designed to take you on a developmental journey to healthy, purpose-driven lives in thirty-six sessions. However, each guide stands on its own and may be taken in any order. You may take a break between studies if you wish.

Who is the leader?

This booklet will walk you through every step for an effective group. In addition, your group may have selected one or more discussion leaders. We strongly recommend that you rotate the job of facilitating your discussions so that everyone's gifts can emerge and develop. You can share other responsibilities as well, such as bringing refreshments or keeping up with those who miss a meeting. There's no reason why one or two people need to do everything; in fact, sharing ownership of the group will help *everyone* grow. Finally, the Bible says that when two or more are gathered in Jesus' name (which you are), he is there in your midst. Ultimately, God is your leader each step of the way.

Where do we find new members for our group?

This can be troubling, especially for new groups that have only a few people or for existing groups that lose a few people along the way. We encourage you to pray with your group and then brainstorm a list of people from work, church, your neighborhood, your children's school, family, the gym, and so forth. Then have each group member invite several of the people on their list. Another good strategy is to ask church leaders to make an announcement or to allow for a bulletin insert.

No matter how you find members, it's vital that you stay on the lookout for new people to join your group. All groups tend to go through some amount of healthy attrition—the result of moves, releasing new leaders, ministry opportunities, and so forth—and if the group gets too small, it could be at risk of shutting down. If you and your group stay open, you'll be amazed at the people God sends your way. The next person just might become a friend for life. You never know!

How do we handle the child care needs in our group?

Very carefully. Seriously, this can be a sensitive issue. We suggest that you empower the group to openly brainstorm solutions. You may try something that works for some and not for others, so you must just keep playing with the dials. One common solution is to meet in the living room or dining room with the adults and to share the cost of a baby-sitter (or two) who can be with the kids in a different part of the house. Another popular option is to use one home for the kids and a second home (close by or a phone call away) for the adults. Finally, you could rotate the responsibility of providing a lesson of some sort for the kids. This last idea can be an incredible blessing to you and the kids. We've done it, and it's worked great! Again, the best approach is to encourage the group to dialogue openly about both the problem and the solution.

APPENDIX

PURPOSE-DRIVEN GROUP AGREEMENT

It's a good idea for every group to put words to their shared values, expectations, and commitments. A written agreement will help you avoid unspoken agendas and disappointed expectations. You'll discuss your agreement in session 1, and then you'll revisit it in session 6 to decide whether you want to modify anything as you move forward as a group. (Alternatively, you may agree to end your group in session 6.) Feel free to modify anything that doesn't work for your group.

If the idea of having a written agreement is unfamiliar to your group, we encourage you to give it a try. A clear agreement is invaluable for resolving conflict constructively and for setting your group on a path to health.

We agree to the following values:

Clear Purpose To grow healthy spiritual lives by building a healthy small group community. In addition, we ___________

____

____

____

____

Group Attendance To give priority to the group meeting (call if I will be late or absent)

Safe Environment To help create a safe place where people can be heard and feel loved (please, no quick answers, snap judgments, or simple fixes)

Confidentiality To keep anything that is shared strictly confidential and within the group

Spiritual Health To give group members permission to help me live a healthy spiritual life that is pleasing to God (see the health assessment and health plan)

Inviting People	To keep an open chair in our group and share Jesus' dream of finding a shepherd for every sheep by inviting newcomers
Shared Ownership	To remember that every member is a minister and to encourage each attender to share a small group role or serve on one of the purpose teams (page 72)
Rotating Leaders	To encourage someone new to facilitate the group each week and to rotate homes and refreshments as well (see Small Group Calendar)
Spiritual Partners	To pair up with one other group member whom I can support more diligently and help to grow spiritually (my spiritual partner is ______________________)

We agree to the following expectations:

- Refreshments/Mealtimes ________________________________
- Child care ____
- When we will meet (day of week) ___________________________
- Where we will meet (place) ______________________________
- We will begin at (time)______________ and end at ______________
- We will do our best to have some or all of us attend a worship service together. Our primary worship service time will be ________________
- Review date of this agreement: ______________________________

We agree to the following commitment:

Father, to the best of my ability, in light of what I know to be true, I commit the next season of my life to CONNECTING with your family, GROWING to be more like Christ, DEVELOPING my shape for ministry, SHARING my life mission every day, and SURRENDERING my life for your pleasure.

______________________________	__________	______________________________
Name	Date	Spiritual Partner (witness)

APPENDIX

SMALL GROUP CALENDAR

Healthy purpose-driven groups share responsibilities and group ownership. This usually doesn't happen overnight but progressively over time. Sharing responsibilities and ownership ensures that no one person carries the group alone. The calendar below can help you in this area. You can also add a social event, mission project, birthdays, or days off to your calendar. This should be completed after your first or second meeting. Planning ahead will facilitate better attendance and greater involvement from others.

Date	Lesson	Location	Dessert/Meal	Facilitator
Monday, January 15	1	Steve and Laura's	Joe	Bill

APPENDIX

PURPOSE TEAM ROLES

The Bible makes clear that every member, not just the small group leader, is a minister in the body of Christ. In a purpose-driven small group (just like in a purpose-driven church), every member plays a role on the team. Review the team roles and responsibilities below and have each member volunteer for a role, or have the group suggest a role for each member. It's best to have one or two people on each team, so you have each purpose covered. Serving in even a small capacity will not only help your leader grow but will also make the group more fun for everyone. Don't hold back. Join a team!

The opportunities below are broken down by the five purposes and then by a *crawl* (beginning group role), *walk* (intermediate group role), or *run* (advanced group role). Try to cover the crawl and walk phases if you can.

Purpose Team Roles		Purpose Team Members
Fellowship Team (**CONNECTING** with God's Family)		
Crawl:	Host social events or group activities	____________
Walk:	Serve as a small group inviter	____________
Run:	Lead the CONNECTING time each week	____________
Discipleship Team (**GROWING** to Be Like Christ)		
Crawl:	Ensure that each member has a simple plan and a partner for personal devotions	____________
Walk:	Disciple a few younger group members	____________
Run:	Facilitate the Purpose-Driven Life Health Assessment and Purpose-Driven Life Health Plan processes	____________

Ministry Team (**DEVELOPING** Your Shape for Ministry)

Crawl:	Ensure that each member finds a group role or a purpose team responsibility	____________
Walk:	Plan a ministry project for the group in the church or community	____________
Run:	Help each member discover and develop a SHAPE-based ministry in the church	____________

Evangelism (Missions) Team (**SHARING** Your Life Mission Every Day)

Crawl:	Coordinate the group prayer and praise list of non-Christian friends and family members	____________
Walk:	Pray for group mission opportunities and plan a group cross-cultural adventure	____________
Run:	Plan as a group to attend a holiday service, host a neighborhood party, or create a seeker event for your non-Christian friends	____________

Worship Team (**SURRENDERING** Your Life for God's Pleasure)

Crawl:	Maintain the weekly group prayer and praise list or journal	____________
Walk:	Lead a brief worship time in your group (CD/video/a cappella)	____________
Run:	Plan a Communion time, prayer walk, foot washing, or an outdoor worship experience	____________

APPENDIX

PURPOSE-DRIVEN LIFE HEALTH ASSESSMENT

	Just Beginning		Getting Going		Well Developed
CONNECTING WITH GOD'S FAMILY					
I am deepening my understanding of and friendship with God in community with others	1	2	3	4	5
I am growing in my ability both to share and to show my love to others	1	2	3	4	5
I am willing to share my real needs for prayer and support from others	1	2	3	4	5
I am resolving conflict constructively and am willing to forgive others	1	2	3	4	5
CONNECTING Total ______					
GROWING TO BE LIKE CHRIST					
I have a growing relationship with God through regular time in the Bible and in prayer (spiritual habits)	1	2	3	4	5
I am experiencing more of the characteristics of Jesus Christ (love, joy, peace, patience, kindness, self-control, etc.) in my life	1	2	3	4	5
I am avoiding addictive behaviors (food, television, busyness, and the like) to meet my needs	1	2	3	4	5
I am spending time with a Christian friend (spiritual partner) who celebrates and challenges my spiritual growth	1	2	3	4	5
GROWING Total ______					
DEVELOPING YOUR SHAPE TO SERVE OTHERS					
I have discovered and am further developing my unique God-given shape for ministry	1	2	3	4	5
I am regularly praying for God to show me opportunities to serve him and others	1	2	3	4	5
I am serving in a regular (once a month or more) ministry in the church or community	1	2	3	4	5
I am a team player in my small group by sharing some group role or responsibility	1	2	3	4	5
DEVELOPING Total______					

	Just Beginning		Getting Going		Well Developed
SHARING YOUR LIFE MISSION EVERY DAY					
I am cultivating relationships with non-Christians and praying for God to give me natural opportunities to share his love	1	2	3	4	5
I am investing my time in another person or group who needs to know Christ personally	1	2	3	4	5
I am regularly inviting unchurched or unconnected friends to my church or small group	1	2	3	4	5
I am praying and learning about where God can use me and our group cross-culturally for missions	1	2	3	4	5
SHARING Total ______					
SURRENDERING YOUR LIFE FOR GOD'S PLEASURE					
I am experiencing more of the presence and power of God in my everyday life	1	2	3	4	5
I am faithfully attending my small group and weekend services to worship God	1	2	3	4	5
I am seeking to please God by surrendering every area of my life (health, decisions, finances, relationships, future, etc.) to him	1	2	3	4	5
I am accepting the things I cannot change and becoming increasingly grateful for the life I've been given	1	2	3	4	5
SURRENDERING Total______					

Total your scores for each purpose, and place them on the chart below. Reassess your progress at the end of thirty days. Be sure to select your spiritual partner and the one area in which you'd like to make progress over the next thirty days.

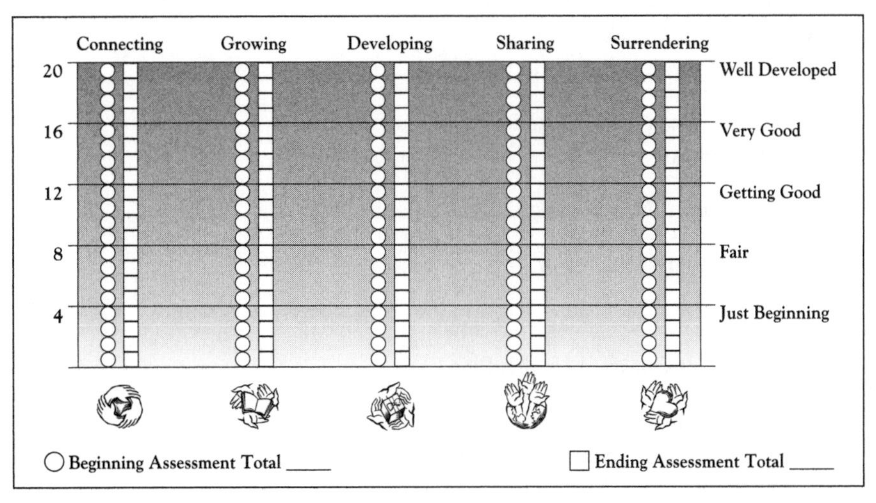

APPENDIX

PURPOSE-DRIVEN LIFE HEALTH PLAN

My Name ______________________________ Date ____________

My Spiritual Partner ______________________________ Date ____________

Possibilities	Plan (make one goal for each area)

CONNECTING WITH GOD'S FAMILY
Hebrews 10:24–25; Ephesians 2:19
How can I deepen my relationships with others?

- Attend my group more faithfully
- Schedule lunch with a group member
- Begin praying for a spiritual mentor

WHO is/are my shepherd(s)?

NAME: ______________________________

GROWING TO BE LIKE CHRIST
Colossians 1:28; Ephesians 4:15
How can I grow to be like Christ?

- Commit to personal time with God three days a week
- Ask a friend for devotional accountability
- Begin journaling my prayers

WHAT is my Spiritual Health Plan?

RENEWAL DATE: ______________________________

DEVELOPING YOUR SHAPE TO SERVE OTHERS

Ephesians 4:11–13; 1 Corinthians 12:7; 1 Peter 3:10

How can I develop my shape for ministry?

- Begin praying for a personal ministry
- Attend a gift discovery class
- Serve together at a church event or in the community

WHERE am I serving others?

MINISTRY: ____________________________

SHARING YOUR LIFE MISSION EVERY DAY

Matthew 28:18–20; Acts 20:24

How can I share my faith every day?

- Start meeting for lunch with a seeker friend
- Invite a non-Christian relative to church
- Pray for and support an overseas missionary

WHEN am I sharing my life mission?

TIME: ________________________________

SURRENDERING YOUR LIFE FOR GOD'S PLEASURE

How can I surrender my life for God's pleasure?

- Submit one area to God
- Be honest about my struggle and hurt
- Buy a music CD for worship in my car and in the group

HOW am I surrendering my life today?

AREA: _______________________________

	Progress (renew and revise)	Progress (renew and revise)	Progress (renew and revise)
	30 days/Date ________ ☐ ☐ ☐ ☐ Weekly check-in with my spiritual partner or group	60-90 days/Date ________ ☐ ☐ ☐ ☐ Weekly check-in with my spiritual partner or group	120+ days/Date ________ ☐ ☐ ☐ ☐ Weekly check-in with my spiritual partner or group
CONNECTING			
GROWING			
DEVELOPING			
SHARING			
SURRENDERING			

APPENDIX

SPIRITUAL PARTNERS' CHECK-IN PAGE

My Name ______________________ Spiritual Partner's Name ______________________

	Our Plans	Our Progress
Week 1		
Week 2		
Week 3		
Week 4		
Week 5		
Week 6		

Briefly check in each week and write down your personal plans and progress for the next week (or even for the next few weeks). This could be done (before or after the meeting) on the phone, through an E-mail message, or even in person from time to time.

APPENDIX

SERVING COMMUNION

Churches vary in their treatment of Communion (the Lord's Supper). Here is one simple form by which a small group can share this experience. You can adapt this form as necessary, depending on your church's beliefs.

Steps in Serving Communion

1. Out of the context of your own experience, say something brief about God's love, forgiveness, grace, mercy, commitment, tenderheartedness, or faithfulness. Connect your words with the personal stories of the group. For example, "These past few weeks I've experienced God's mercy in the way he untangled the situation with my son. And I've seen God show mercy to others of us here too, especially to Jean and Roger." If you prefer, you can write down ahead of time what you want to say.

2. Read 1 Corinthians 11:23–26:

   The Lord Jesus, on the night he was betrayed, took bread, [24]and when he had given thanks, he broke it and said, "This is my body, which is for you; do this in remembrance of me." [25]In the same way, after supper he took the cup, saying, "This cup is the new covenant in my blood; do this, whenever you drink it, in remembrance of me." [26]For whenever you eat this bread and drink this cup, you proclaim the Lord's death until he comes.

3. Pray silently and pass the bread around the circle. While the bread is being passed, you may want to reflect quietly, sing a simple praise song, or listen to a worship tape.

4. When everyone has received the bread, remind them that this represents Jesus' broken body on their behalf. Simply state, "Jesus said, 'Do this in remembrance of me.' Let us eat together," and eat the bread as a group.

5. Pray silently and serve the cup. You may pass a small tray, serve people individually, or have them pick up a cup from the table.

6. When everyone has been served, remind them that the cup represents Jesus' blood shed for them. Simply state, "The cup of the new covenant is Jesus Christ's blood shed for you. Jesus said, 'Do this in remembrance of me.' Let us drink together." Then drink the juice as a group.
7. Conclude by singing a simple song, listening to a praise song, or having a time of prayer in thanks to God.

Practical Tips in Serving Communion

1. Prepare the elements simply, sacredly, and symbolically.
2. Be sensitive to timing in your meeting.
3. Break up pieces of cracker or soft bread on a small plate or tray. *Don't* use large servings of bread or grape juice. We encourage you to use grape juice, not wine, because wine is a cause of stumbling for some people.
4. Have all of the elements prepared beforehand, and just bring them into the room or to the table when you are ready.

☐ **For Further Study**

Other Communion passages: Matthew 26:26–29; Mark 14:22–25; Luke 22:14–20; 1 Corinthians 10:16–21; 11:17–34

APPENDIX

MEMORY VERSES

One of the most effective ways to instill biblical truth deep into our lives is to memorize key Scriptures. For many, memorization is a new concept—or perhaps one we found difficult in the past. We encourage you to stretch yourself and try to memorize these six verses.

A good way to memorize a verse is to copy it on a sheet of paper five times. Most people learn something by heart when they do this. It's also helpful to post the verse someplace where you will see it several times a day.

WEEK ONE

"Seek first his kingdom and his righteousness, and all these things will be given to you as well."

Matthew 6:33

WEEK TWO

"I pray that out of his glorious riches he may strengthen you with power through his Spirit in your inner being, so that Christ may dwell in your hearts through faith."

Ephesians 3:16–17

WEEK THREE

"You are worried and upset about many things, but only one thing is needed. Mary has chosen what is better, and it will not be taken away from her."

Luke 10:41–42

WEEK FOUR

"Be still and know that I am God;
I will be exalted among the nations,
I will be exalted in the earth."

Psalm 46:10

WEEK FIVE

"Do your best to present yourself to God as one approved, a workman who does not need to be ashamed and who correctly handles the word of truth."

2 Timothy 2:15

WEEK SIX

"Consider it pure joy, my brothers, whenever you face trials of many kinds, because you know that the testing of your faith develops perseverance."

James 1:2–3

APPENDIX

DAILY DEVOTIONAL READINGS

We've experienced so much life change as a result of reading the Bible daily. Hundreds of people have gone through DOING LIFE TOGETHER, and they tell us that the number-one contributor to their growth was the deeper walk with God that came as a result of the daily devotions. We strongly encourage you to have everyone set a realistic goal for the six weeks. Pair people into same-gender spiritual (accountability) partners. This will improve your results tenfold. Then we encourage everyone to take a few minutes each day to **READ** the verse for the day, **REFLECT** on what God is saying to you through the verse, and **RESPOND** to God in prayer in a personal journal. Each of these verses was selected to align with the week's study. After you complete the reading, simply put a check mark in the box next to the verse. Enjoy the journey!

WEEK ONE

- ☐ 2 Corinthians 3:18
- ☐ Philippians 3:13–14
- ☐ 1 Thessalonians 3:9–13
- ☐ Colossians 1:28
- ☐ Colossians 1:9–10

WEEK TWO

- ☐ 1 Corinthians 3:16–17
- ☐ Ephesians 5:18–21
- ☐ 2 Corinthians 3:17–18
- ☐ Romans 8:15–17
- ☐ 1 Corinthians 2:12–16

WEEK THREE

- ☐ Psalm 42:1
- ☐ Psalm 37:4–5
- ☐ Psalm 138:8
- ☐ Psalm 145:17–19
- ☐ Isaiah 50:4–5

WEEK FOUR

- ☐ John 16:23–24
- ☐ Philippians 4:6–7
- ☐ Proverbs 15:29
- ☐ 1 Thessalonians 5:16–18
- ☐ James 5:16–18

WEEK FIVE

- ☐ Psalm 1:1–3
- ☐ Isaiah 55:1–3
- ☐ 2 Timothy 3:16–17
- ☐ Psalm 19:7–11
- ☐ Hebrews 4:12–13

WEEK SIX

- ☐ 1 Corinthians 10:13
- ☐ Psalm 40:1–3
- ☐ Philippians 4:8–9
- ☐ 2 Corinthians 4:16–18
- ☐ Romans 8:38–39

APPENDIX

PRAYER AND PRAISE REPORT

Briefly share your prayer requests with the large group, making notations below. Then gather in small groups of two, three, or four to pray for each need.

	Prayer Request	Praise Report
Week 1		
Week 2		
Week 3		

	Prayer Request	Praise Report
Week 4		
Week 5		
Week 6		

SAMPLE JOURNAL PAGE

Today's Passage: ______________________________

Reflections from my HEART:

I ***H**onor* who you are. (Praise God for something.)

I ***E**xpress* who I'm not. (Confess any known sin.)

I ***A**ffirm* who I am in you. (How does God see you?)

I ***R**equest* your will for me. (Ask God for something.)

I ***T**hank* you for what you've done. (Thank him for something.)

Today's Action Step:

LEADERSHIP TRAINING

Small Group Leadership 101 (Top Ten Ideas for New Facilitators)

Congratulations! You have responded to the call to help shepherd Jesus' flock. There are few other tasks in the family of God that surpass the contribution you will be making. As you prepare to lead—whether it is one session or the entire series—here are a few thoughts to keep in mind. We encourage you to read these and review them with each new discussion leader before he or she leads.

1. **Remember that you are not alone.** God knows everything about you, and he knew that you would be asked to lead your group. Even though you may not feel ready to lead, this is common for all good leaders. Moses, Solomon, Jeremiah, or Timothy—they *all* were reluctant to lead. God promises, "Never will I leave you; never will I forsake you" (Hebrews 13:5). Whether you are leading for one evening, for several weeks, or for a lifetime, you will be blessed as you serve.

2. **Don't try to do it alone.** Pray right now for God to help you build a healthy leadership team. If you can enlist a coleader to help you lead the group, you will find your experience to be much richer. This is your chance to involve as many people as you can in building a healthy group. All you have to do is call and ask people to help—you'll be surprised at the response.

3. **Just be yourself.** If you won't be you, who will? God wants to use your unique gifts and temperament. Don't try to do things exactly like another leader; do them in a way that fits you! Just admit it when you don't have an answer and apologize when you make a mistake. Your group will love you for it!—and you'll sleep better at night.

4. **Prepare for your meeting ahead of time.** Review the session and the leader's notes, and write down your responses to each question. Pay special attention to exercises that ask group members to do something other than engage in discussion. These exercises will help your group *live* what the Bible teaches, not just talk about it. Be sure you understand how an exercise works, and bring any necessary supplies (such as paper or pens) to your meeting. If the exercise employs one of the items in the appendix (such as the Purpose-Driven Life Health Assessment), be sure to look over that item so you'll know

how it works. Finally, review "Read Me First" on pages 11–14 so you'll remember the purpose of each section in the study.

5. **Pray for your group members by name.** Before you begin your session, go around the room in your mind and pray for each member by name. You may want to review the prayer list at least once a week. Ask God to use your time together to touch the heart of every person uniquely. Expect God to lead you to whomever he wants you to encourage or challenge in a special way. If you listen, God will surely lead!

6. **When you ask a question, be patient.** Someone will eventually respond. Sometimes people need a moment or two of silence to think about the question, and if silence doesn't bother you, it won't bother anyone else. After someone responds, affirm the response with a simple "thanks" or "good job." Then ask, "How about somebody else?" or "Would someone who hasn't shared like to add anything?" Be sensitive to new people or reluctant members who aren't ready to say, pray, or do anything. If you give them a safe setting, they will blossom over time.

7. **Provide transitions between questions.** When guiding the discussion, always read aloud the transitional paragraphs and the questions. Ask the group if anyone would like to read the paragraph or Bible passage. Don't call on anyone, but ask for a volunteer, and then be patient until someone begins. Be sure to thank the person who reads aloud.

8. **Break up into small groups each week, or they won't stay.** If your group has more than seven people, we strongly encourage you to have the group gather in discussion circles of three or four people during the GROWING or SURRENDERING sections of the study. With a greater opportunity to talk in a small circle, people will connect more with the study, apply more quickly what they're learning, and ultimately get more out of it. A small circle also encourages a quiet person to participate and tends to minimize the effects of a more vocal or dominant member. And it can help people feel more loved in your group. When you gather again at the end of the section, you can have one person summarize the highlights from each circle.

Small circles are also helpful during prayer time. People who are unaccustomed to praying aloud will feel more comfortable trying it with just two or three others. Also, prayer requests won't take as much time, so circles will have more time to actually pray. When you gather back with the whole group, you can have one person from each circle briefly update everyone on the prayer requests. People are more willing to pray in small circles if they know that the whole group will hear all the prayer requests.

9. **Rotate facilitators weekly.** At the end of each meeting, ask the group who should lead the following week. Let the group help select your weekly facilitator. You may be perfectly capable of leading each time, but you will help others grow in their faith and gifts if you give them opportunities to lead. You can use the Small Group Calendar on page 71 to fill in the names of all six meeting leaders at once if you prefer.

10. **One final challenge (for new or first-time leaders): Before your first opportunity to lead, look up each of the five passages listed below.** Read each one as a devotional exercise to help prepare yourself with a shepherd's heart. Trust us on this one. If you do this, you will be more than ready for your first meeting.

- ☐ Matthew 9:36
- ☐ 1 Peter 5:2-4
- ☐ Psalm 23
- ☐ Ezekiel 34:11–16
- ☐ 1 Thessalonians 2:7–8, 11–12

Small Group Leadership Lifters (Weekly Leadership Tips)

And David shepherded them with integrity of heart;
with skillful hands he led them.

Psalm 78:73

David provides a model of a leader who has a heart for God, a desire to shepherd God's people, and a willingness to develop the skills of a leader. The following is a series of practical tips for new and existing small group leaders. These principles and practices have proved to cultivate healthy, balanced groups in over a thousand examples.

1. Don't Leave Home without It: A Leader's Prayer

"The prayer of a righteous man [or woman] is powerful and effective" (James 5:16). From the very beginning of this study, why not commit to a simple prayer of renewal in your heart and in the hearts of your members? Take a moment right now and write a simple prayer as you begin:

Father, help me ____

____

____

2. Pay It Now or Pay It Later: Group Conflict

Most leaders and groups avoid conflict, but healthy groups are willing to do what it takes to learn and grow through conflict. Much group conflict can be avoided if the leader lets the group openly discuss and decide its direction, using the Purpose-Driven Group Agreement. Healthy groups are alive. Conflict is a sign of maturity, not mistakes. Sometimes you may need to get outside counsel, but don't be afraid. See conflict as an opportunity to grow, and always confront it so it doesn't create a cancer that can kill the group over time (Matthew 18:15–20).

3. Lead from Weakness

The apostle Paul said that God's power was made perfect in Paul's weakness (2 Corinthians 12:9). This is clearly the opposite of what most leaders think, but it provides the most significant model of humility, authority, and spiritual power. It was Jesus' way at the cross. So share your struggles along with your successes, confess your sins to one another along with your celebrations, and ask for prayer for yourself along with praying for others. God will be pleased, and your group will grow deeper. If you humble yourself under God's mighty hand, he will exalt you at the proper time (Matthew 23:12).

4. What Makes Jesus Cry: A Leader's Focus

In Matthew 9:35–38, Jesus looked at the crowds following him and saw them as sheep without a shepherd. He was moved with compassion, because they were "distressed and downcast" (NASB); the NIV says they were "harassed and helpless." The Greek text implies that he was moved to the point of tears.

Never forget that you were once one of those sheep yourself. We urge you to keep yourself and your group focused not just inwardly to each other but also outwardly to people beyond your group. Jesus said, "Follow me ... and I will make you fishers of men" (Matthew 4:19). We assume that you and your group are following him. So how is your fishing going? As leader, you can ignite in your group Jesus' compassion for outsiders. For his sake, keep the fire burning!

5. Prayer Triplets

Prayer triplets can provide a rich blessing to you and many others. At the beginning or end of your group meeting, you can gather people into prayer triplets to share and pray about three non-Christian friends. This single strategy will increase your group's evangelistic effectiveness considerably. Be sure to get an update on the plans and progress from each of the circles. You need only ten minutes at every other meeting—but do this at least once a month. At first, some of your members may feel overwhelmed at the thought of praying for non-Christians. We've been there! But you can be confident that over time they will be renewed in their heart for lost people and experience the blessing of giving birth to triplets.

6. Race against the Clock

When your group grows in size or your members begin to feel more comfortable talking, you will inevitably feel as though you're racing against the clock. You may know the feeling very well. The good news is that there are several simple things that can help your group stick to your agreed schedule:

- The time crunch is actually a sign of relational and spiritual health, so pat yourselves on the back.
- Check in with the group to problem-solve, because they feel the tension as well.
- You could begin your meeting a little early or ask for a later ending time.
- If you split up weekly into circles of three to four people for discussion, you will double the amount of time any one person can share.

- Appoint a timekeeper to keep the group on schedule.
- Remind everyone to give brief answers.
- Be selective in the number of questions you try to discuss.
- Finally, planning the time breaks in your booklet before the group meeting begins can really keep you on track.

7. All for One and One for All: Building a Leadership Team

The statement "Together Everybody Accomplishes More" (TEAM) is especially true in small groups. The Bible clearly teaches that every member is a minister. Be sure to empower the group to share weekly facilitation, as well as other responsibilities, and seek to move every player onto a team over time. Don't wait for people to ask, because it just won't happen. From the outset of your group, try to get everybody involved. The best way to get people in the game is to have the group suggest who would serve best on what team and in what role. See Purpose Team Roles on pages 72–73 for several practical suggestions. You could also talk to people individually or ask for volunteers in the group, but don't miss this opportunity to develop every group member and build a healthy and balanced group over time.

8. Purpose-Driven Groups Produce Purpose-Driven Lives: A Leader's Goal

As you undertake this new curriculum, especially if this is your first time as a leader, make sure you begin with the end in mind. You may have heard the phrase, "If you aim at nothing, you'll hit it every time." It's vital for your group members to review their spiritual health by using the Purpose-Driven Life Health Assessment and Purpose-Driven Life Health Plan (pages 74–78). You'll do part of the health assessment in your group in session 2 and share your results with spiritual partners for support and accountability. Each member will also set one goal for thirty days. The goal will be tied to the purpose you are studying in this particular guide. We strongly encourage you to go even further and do the entire health assessment together. Then during another group session (or on their own), members can set a goal for each of the other four purposes.

Pairing up with spiritual partners will offer invaluable support for that area of personal growth. Encourage partners to pray for one another in the area of their goals. Have partners gather at least three times during the series to share their progress and plans. This will give you and the group the best results. In order for people to follow through with their goals, you'll need to lead with vision and modeling. Share your goals with the group, and update them on how the steps you're taking have been affecting your spiritual life. If you share your progress and plans, others will follow in your footsteps.

9. Discover the Power of Pairs

The best resolutions get swept aside by busyness and forgetfulness, which is why it's important for group members to have support as they pursue a spiritual goal. Have them pair up with spiritual partners in session 2, or encourage them to seek out a Christian coworker or personal mentor. You can promise that they'll never be the same if they simply commit to supporting each other with prayer and encouragement on a weekly basis.

It's best to start with one goal in an area of greatest need. Most of the time the area will be either evangelism or consistent time with the Father in prayer and in Scripture reading. Cultivating time with God is the place to start; if group members are already doing this, they can move on to a second and third area of growth.

You just need a few victories in the beginning. Have spiritual partners check in together at the beginning or end of each group meeting. Ask them to support those check-ins with phone calls, coffee times, and E-mail messages during the week. Trust us on this one—you will see people grow like never before.

10. Don't Lose Heart: A Leader's Vision

You are a strategic player in the heavenly realm. Helping a few others grow in Christ could put you squarely in the sights of Satan himself. First Corinthians 15:58 (NASB) says, "Be steadfast, immovable, always abounding in the work of the Lord." Leading a group is not always going to be easy. Here are the keys to longevity and lasting joy as a leader:

- Be sure to refuel your soul as you give of yourself to others. We recommend that you ask a person to meet with you for personal coaching and encouragement. When asked (over coffee or lunch) to support someone in leadership, nine out of ten people say, "I'd love to!" So why not ask?
- Delegate responsibilities after the first meeting. Doing so will help group members grow, and it will give you a break as well.
- Most important, cultivating your own walk with God puts you on the offensive against Satan and increases the joy zone for everyone in your life. Make a renewed decision right now to make this happen. Don't give Satan a foothold in your heart; there is simply too much at stake.

LEADER'S NOTES

SESSION ONE: GROWING DEEPER IN CHRIST

Goals of the Session

- To encourage you to grow deeper in your spiritual journey
- To understand what running the race with Jesus involves
- To commit to some basic shared values of your group

Especially helpful for this session: Leadership Lifters #1 and #4

Before you meet for the first time, invite as many people as you would enjoy hanging out with. It just makes the group a whole lot more fun for you as the leader. Also, ask one or two people if they'd be willing to colead with you so you don't have to do it alone.

Open your meeting with a brief prayer.

Question 1. As leader, you should be the first to answer this question. Your answer will model the amount of time and vulnerability you want others to imitate. If you are brief, others will be brief. If your answer is superficial, you'll set a superficial tone—but if you tell something substantive and personal, others will know that your group is a safe place to tell the truth about themselves.

Be sure to give each person a chance to respond to this question, because it's an opportunity for group members to get to know each other. It's not necessary to go around the circle in order. People may have trouble limiting their answers to one minute. That's fine in a first session when everyone is getting to know each other. The CONNECTING portion of your meeting will be briefer in future sessions. If yours is a new group, it's especially important to allow extra time for people to share their personal stories. Everyone needs to feel known so that they feel they belong. The sharing of stories may decrease the available time for Bible study, but this will be time well spent in the early weeks of a group's life. And even if your group has been meeting together for some time, you will find that the CONNECTING questions will help you understand one another better and enrich your Bible study.

Introduction to the Series. If this is your first study guide in the DOING LIFE TOGETHER series, you'll need to take time after question 1 to orient the group to one principle that undergirds the series: *A healthy purpose-driven small group balances the five purposes of the church in order to help people balance them in their lives*. Most small groups emphasize Bible study, fellowship, and prayer. But God has called us to reach out to others as well. If the five purposes are new to your group, be sure to review the Read Me First section with your new group. In addition, the Frequently Asked Questions section could help your group understand some of the purpose-driven group basics.

Question 2. If your group has done another study guide in the DOING LIFE TOGETHER series within the past six months, you may not need to go over the Purpose-Driven Group Agreement again. It's a good idea to remind people of the agreement from time to time, but for an established group, recommitting every six months is reasonable. If you're new to the series and if you don't already have a group agreement, turn to page 69 and take about ten minutes to look at the Purpose-Driven Group Agreement. Read each value aloud in turn, and let group members comment at the end. Emphasize confidentiality—a commitment that is essential to the ability to trust each other.

"Spiritual Health" says that group members give permission to encourage each other to set spiritual goals *for themselves*. As the study progresses, a group member may set a goal to do daily devotions, or a dad may set a goal to spend half an hour each evening with his children. No one will set goals for someone else; each person will be free to set his or her own goals.

"Shared Ownership" points toward session 3, when members will be asked to help with some responsibility in the group. It may be as simple as bringing refreshments or keeping track of prayer requests. Ultimately, it's healthy for groups to rotate leadership among several, or perhaps even all, members. People grow when they contribute. However, no one should feel pressured into a responsibility.

Regarding expectations: It's amazing how many groups never take the time to make explicit plans about refreshments, child care, and other such issues. Child care is a big issue in many groups. It's important to treat it as an issue that the group as a whole needs to solve, even if the group decides that each member will make arrangements separately.

If you feel that your group needs to move on, you can save the conversation about expectations until the end of your meeting.

Question 3. Have someone read the Bible passage aloud. It's a good idea to ask someone ahead of time, because not everyone is comfortable reading aloud in public. When the passage has been read, ask question 3. Don't be afraid to allow silence while people think. It's completely normal to have periods of silence in a Bible study. You might count to seven silently. If nobody says anything, say something humorous like, "I can wait longer than you can!" It's not necessary that everyone respond to every one of the Bible study questions.

Question 4. Believing in Jesus Christ is enough to get to heaven. But if you believe but don't act on your beliefs, you're sitting on the bench when you should be running. Taking action to know, hear, and obey Jesus is what makes you a runner. God doesn't want anybody on the bench. He wants everybody on the field. Salvation is a free gift of God's grace. Yet, grace is opposed to earning, not effort. As you'll see in session 2, the power that fuels your effort is also a gift of grace.

Don't forget to give encouragement when people offer answers. Even if someone's answer is difficult to understand, remember that it takes a tremendous step of faith, especially in new groups, to say something early on. Say something like, "Great!" "Thanks!" "That's super." Then say, "How about somebody else?" "Does anybody else want to share?" Especially if someone starts to dominate the discussion, say, "How about somebody who hasn't shared yet?" Keep these things bouncing back and forth.

Question 10. The open chair is a vivid symbol of one of the values in the Purpose-Driven Group Agreement—"Inviting People." Some groups fear that newcomers will interrupt the intimacy that members have built over time. However, groups that use the empty chair generally gain strength with the infusion of new blood. It's like a river of living water flowing into a stagnant pond. Some groups remain permanently open, while others choose to open periodically, such as at the beginning and ending of a study.

Give people a quiet moment or two in which to write down a name. Then have them share the names. You might pray for these names later in your session. Encourage people not to be afraid to ask others into the group.

Question 11. In session 3 you'll talk about the value of spending daily time with God. The devotional passages on page 83 give your group a chance to test-drive this spiritual discipline. Encourage everyone to give it a try. There are five short readings for each session, so people can read one a day and even skip a couple of days a week. Talk to your group about committing to reading and reflecting on these verses each day. This practice has revolutionized the spiritual lives of others who have used this study, so we highly recommend it. There will be an opportunity in future sessions to share what you have discovered in your devotional reading. Remind group members of the sample journal page on page 86.

Beginning in session 2, people will have an opportunity to check in with one other member at the end of several of the group sessions to share what they learned from the Lord in their devotional time.

Question 12. Some groups really enjoy the chance to hear each person's prayer request in full detail. However, if your group is larger than six people, doing so can take considerable time. Smaller prayer circles give people more airtime to share their requests, as well as a less intimidating setting in which to take their first steps in praying aloud. If your group feels strongly about hearing everyone's requests, you can ask one person in each small circle to be the recorder and write down the requests. After the circles have finished praying, the recorder from each circle can briefly report the requests to the group. Members who want to hear the whole story can ask each other after the meeting.

You are the expert about your group. If your members are seasoned veterans in group prayer, let them go for it. But if you have members who are new believers, new to small groups, or just new to praying aloud, suggest an option that will feel comfortable for them. Newcomers won't come back if they find themselves in the scary position of having to pray aloud as "perfectly" as the veterans. Talking to God is more significant than talking to your nation's president or to a movie star—so it's no wonder people feel intimidated! A silent prayer, a one-sentence prayer, or even a one-word prayer are completely acceptable first steps. Make sure the circles understand this so that no one feels he or she is being put on the spot.

As you end your group time, be sure to pass the leadership to your coleader for the following week. Encourage him or her to read through the leadership sections in preparation for next week's study.

If you have an existing group, some group members may resist structural change—or any kind of change for that matter. Encourage them to test-drive the new format with an open mind, and see what God may do. You never know—it may generate fresh gusts of wind for the sails of your group.

SESSION TWO: THE POWER FOR LIVING

Goals of the Session

- To discover how to access the power of the Holy Spirit
- To learn how to practice spiritual breathing (moment by moment)
- To make a plan for spiritual growth over the next thirty days

Especially helpful for this session: Leadership Lifters #3 and #6

New rotating leaders may want to meet ahead of time with an experienced leader to review the plan for the meeting. You may want to have some extra booklets on hand for any new group members.

Question 1. Give some thought ahead of time to an answer for this question. Think of something that will give people a glimpse into an area of your need for God, not something that will make you sound superspiritual. This is a chance for you to set a tone of openness and vulnerability toward God.

Questions 2–3. Give people a minute or two on their own to do questions 2 and 3. Don't make them share their answers.

Question 4. It's hard to break the habits listed in the left-hand column because they're so deeply ingrained. They may be considered "normal" with regard to our families or to the people we've lived among for years. They may be strategies we developed in order to survive painful situations when we didn't know that we should have turned to the Holy Spirit. We may even have been born with a vulnerability to alcoholism, a predisposition to a volatile temper, or a tendency toward anxiety or some other weakness. Sexual integrity doesn't come naturally. Neither does contentment. Trusting the Spirit to lead us often feels extremely unnatural until we've been immersed in it for a long time and have seen demonstrations of God's faithfulness and power.

Question 5. Let's say you have a habit of gossiping. Talking about others makes you feel connected to your friends. Yielding to the Holy Spirit may involve, first of all, hearing him say, through the words of the Bible, that gossiping is wrong and destructive. An important part of yielding is acknowledging that you do, in fact, participate in gossip, and you like doing so. You begin, then, to humble yourself, admitting that you don't have the power on your own to stop gossiping. You make time to think about why you gossip. You listen when the Spirit points out that what you really want is the feeling of connection; gossiping is simply a means to that end. You pray for the power to change. You may ask someone to support you in prayer. You give the Spirit permission to alert you in the middle of conversations to instances of gossiping. When you notice that you're gossiping, you acknowledge your sin. You say to the other person, "Can we talk about something else?" You do so over and over, and the habit begins to break.

This is one person's example. Yielding may look very different for you.

Question 7. You might write, "I would give up gossiping for a God who loves me so much that I don't need to build myself up by tearing others down."

Knowing that you're genuinely and passionately loved clears away things that can block you from following Jesus—things such as fear of failure, fear of looking ridiculous, fear of retaliation from another person, selfish ambition, envy, ego, lust, and greed. If you know you're loved, the commitment to gaining more and more money or to looking good just doesn't matter as much. In this way, God's love motivates you to choose the fruit of the Spirit rather than the deeds of the flesh.

Question 8. Familiarize yourself with this exercise before your meeting. When you come to this point in the meeting, simply read aloud the instructions in a slow, steady voice while the rest of the group does what the instructions say. Read the prayer with a reverent attitude. Allow a few seconds of silence before inviting group members to open their eyes. You can encourage people to talk about their responses to this exercise. Don't worry if some people express disdain. Some personalities don't care for this kind of activity, while others gravitate toward it. This study attempts to provide a variety of experiences for a variety of learning styles, so no one activity will appeal equally to every person.

Even though it may seem trite to do this kind of breathing exercise, the Spirit-filled life is very similar to breathing. Living out the Christian life in a Spirit-led way is a moment-by-moment action, just like breathing. We humbly give our sin over to the Lord (exhaling), and we breathe in desires and love that are of the Spirit (inhaling).

Question 9. Familiarize yourself with the Purpose-Driven Life Health Assessment before the meeting. You may want to take the assessment yourself ahead of time and think about your goal. Then you can give group members a real-life example of what you are actually committed to doing. We also encourage you to complete a simple goal under each purpose. Ask your coleader or a trusted friend to review it with you. Then you'll understand the power of this tool and the support you can gain from a spiritual partner.

Offer this health assessment in a spirit of grace. It should make people hungry to see the Holy Spirit work in their lives, not ashamed that they're falling short. Nobody can do these things in the power of the flesh! And sometimes the most mature believers have the clearest perception of the areas in which they need considerable help from the Spirit.

Question 10. Help guide people to pair up with partners with whom they will have a good chemistry. Spiritual partnership works best when people trust each other. Point out the Spiritual Partners' Check-In Page on page 79, which can give partners a structure for checking in with each other. Bear in mind that some personalities love self-assessments and setting goals, while others are more resistant. Some people who routinely set goals at work may be taken aback at the idea of setting a goal for their spiritual lives. Assure everyone that their goals can be small steps, that no one will be pressured into performing or humiliated for falling short, and that God is always eager to give grace.

The Purpose-Driven Life Health Plan on pages 76–78 is a tool to help people be more focused in setting goals for spiritual health. It contains suggested goals, questions to think about, and a chart for keeping track of feedback from spiritual partners. Point it out and encourage group members to use it if it seems helpful. You may also want to consult your Small Group Calendar (page 71) to see who might lead your discussion next time. Finally, go to the Purpose Team worksheet and encourage each person to prayerfully consider which team or role he or she would like to share in the following week.

SESSION THREE: PERSONAL TIME WITH GOD

Goals of the Session

- To understand what it means to have a personal time with God
- To experience a personal time with God during the group time
- To take a step toward balancing the five purposes in the group

Especially helpful for this session: Leadership Lifters #7 and #8

Question 3. The purpose of this question is to allow the Martha voice in each of you to have its say. When we study this passage, we often jump right to the clear point that Jesus is making: *No matter how important our daily tasks seem to be, nothing is more important than spending time sitting at Jesus' feet.* It's easy to affirm this message—but then to go right back to doing life as usual. Why do we do that? Because we haven't really addressed the very sensible voice of Martha, who says such things as, "It's great to sit at your feet, Lord—but doesn't somebody have to get dinner on the table? If I sit by you, everyone's going to be on my case later on, complaining that they're hungry. Maybe you don't think all this work on my plate is very important, but the rest of the people in my life expect me to get it done!"

Take some time to vent these Martha arguments. How do people expect you to spend your time? Who are the people whose expectations weigh heaviest on you? What do you imagine would happen if you set these expectations aside for a half hour each day? Then discuss what you think Jesus would say in response to these arguments.

Questions 8–9. Having discussed the value of personal time with God, you now have an exercise that allows group members to experience it. Some people learn better by *experiencing* something than by talking about it. If every person in your group already takes time for God each day and doesn't want to learn another method, you can skip this exercise. But if you have any group members who still aren't consistent in their time with God, ask *everyone* to do the exercise. Members who already take time for God can help beginners by genuinely doing the exercise and then sharing what they gained from God's Word—even in the course of a ten-minute time period. As leader, you can set an example. Don't just go through the motions of a devotional time;

allow God to speak to you anew through the Scriptures and then share something genuine and personal that you discovered.

If you're running out of time, you can have people respond to question 9 with just one sentence or with a one-word reaction to the experience. You might ask something like, "How would you describe this experience, using just a single word?"

Question 10. Here is an opportunity for members to begin to share ownership of the group. Some groups expect the leader to do everything, but healthy groups come to share responsibilities over time. By taking on small tasks like these, members will also discover and develop their gifts and interests with regard to serving others. Experimenting with acts of service will eventually help people identify how God has uniquely designed them for ministry. The suggested tasks are only ideas. Encourage group members to decide for themselves what would be good ways to serve the group. Ideally, get the group to go to the Purpose Team sheet (page 72). This will give a comprehensive understanding of the concept. You want to move forward with the presumption that each member will participate on a team or fill a role.

Question 11. This conversation could take twenty minutes. It's intended, though, to take just five minutes. If your time is limited, encourage spiritual partners to connect with each other after the meeting.

SESSION FOUR: ENTERING GOD'S PRESENCE

Goals of the Session

- To understand Jesus' desire for how we should pray
- To provide a safe place in which to share struggles and find support
- To explore some ways to develop meaningful prayer

Especially helpful for this session: Leadership Lifters #8

Question 2. One tip: *Private prayer is extremely valuable to your spiritual growth*. Another tip: *Don't pray in order to be seen by others*. When Jesus tells us to pray in secret, he doesn't mean he's against praying in a group. Rather, he wants you to forget about the human audience when you pray in your group. It doesn't matter if they think you sound good. You have an audience of one—your heavenly Father. A third tip: *Quantity doesn't count*. One heartfelt, honest sentence is more of a "real" prayer than ten minutes of talk that doesn't lay your heart bare before the Lord.

Question 4. Focusing first of all on God's greatness builds your faith by reminding you that God has all power and all love to give you the very best. It puts your life and problems into perspective. It puts God first, where he belongs. And it establishes that you are not just whining or giving a speech; you are connecting with a Person.

Questions 6–7. It's not necessary for each person to answer question 6. But do encourage everyone to answer question 7. If you're in a small circle of three or four, it won't take long to pray for each person. Also, your prayer time at the end of the meeting will be briefer because you're praying for each other now.

Question 10. If you're in small circles, the leader of the whole group may need to flag everyone when it's time to write out a prayer. You can assign just five minutes to this exercise if your time is running out. It's not necessary for people to write something in each category—someone might want to spend the entire five minutes writing an expression of praise to God for one of his qualities. The point of this exercise is to give people an opportunity to come up with some genuine words to say to God. Many people find it easier to do this on paper than to try to say it aloud. Even people who are very experienced with prayer find that writing down a prayer adds a new dimension to their prayer lives.

Question 12. Read the instructions for Communion ahead of time so you're prepared for this discussion. Sharing Communion in a small group isn't difficult—why not give it a try? You can spread around the tasks of providing bread, juice, a plate, and cups. This discussion doesn't need to take more than just a couple of minutes.

LEADER'S NOTES

SESSION FIVE: A TASTE FOR GOD'S WORD

Goals of the Session

- To motivate you to begin studying God's Word on your own
- To experience a simple model for personal Bible study
- To discover how to study your Bible regularly

Especially helpful for this session: Leadership Lifters #4 and #5

Questions 3-5. This exercise is written for people who have never done Bible study before. However, those who have had a lot of experience with Bible study may be surprised at how much they can get out of a passage by taking the time to make fresh observations. Not everyone enjoys this kind of study, but it's helpful to know how to do it.

You should watch the time. After five minutes, encourage people to move on to interpretation even if they haven't made all possible observations. After another five minutes, ask them to move on to application.

For this particular passage from Philippians, who, what, how, and why will be the most important observations. Where and when are more important for other passages, though, so it's a good idea to think about each type of question with every passage, just to see what comes up.

The same as is a key phrase for the interpretation phase. It's a clue to this passage's main point—a comparison between our approach to life and Jesus' approach, which should be the same. The repeated words *humility, humbled,* and *servant* underline what this approach is: *Jesus approached life as a humble servant, so we aren't endangering our self-esteem if we do the same.* This passage flies in the face of the pop-psychology belief that if you want to be healthy, you need to put yourself first. If someone raises the question of codependency, you might comment that serving others is not the same as doing whatever they want so that they'll love you. Codependency is a distortion of service, because it's rooted in the fear of abandonment or of punishment. Real service attends to others' genuine needs, not simply to their demands.

Question 6. You'll probably get a range of responses, from "that was great!" to "I don't get it." Affirm those who find Bible study difficult. They are undoubtedly stronger in certain other areas. See if the group can answer each other's questions.

Question 9. Communion will probably take ten minutes if you have everything prepared ahead of time. It's a tremendously moving experience in a small group. Not all churches want their small groups to do Communion on their own, so if you're in doubt, be sure to check with your leadership.

LEADER'S NOTES

SESSION SIX: THE UNLIKELY ROUTE TO JOY

Goals of the Session

- To understand how God uses trials to help us become what we were created to be
- To support members who may be dealing with trials right now
- To celebrate the end of this six-week study and make decisions about what's next for you

Especially helpful for this session: Leadership Lifters #2 and #10

Question 1. You should be the first to give your responses here. Think about your answers ahead of time so you can share something genuine, substantive, and warm. You'll set the tone for everyone else. It's important not to be superficial or too general when affirming your group's strengths. Thinking ahead will also help you keep your response concise so that others will try to be concise as well.

Question 2. Trials test our faith, develop perseverance, and help us become mature.

Question 3. Several answers are possible. One is that perseverance seems to be a foundational quality for character or virtue. Without perseverance, the aspects of the fruit of the Spirit (love, joy, peace, and so forth) are flighty and unreliable and susceptible to crumbling under pressure. Perseverance is what gives backbone to our expression of the fruit of the Spirit and helps us avoid hard-heartedness.

Question 4. It would be easy for a discussion of hardships to become a downer. That's undesirable for your last session in the series. It would be equally easy for a discussion of hardships to be superficial, with everyone insisting they're oh-so-joyful when in reality life is awfully hard. Your task is to steer a middle course of clarity about the upside that there is to down times, along with honesty about how hard it often is to rejoice in trials. If others seem reluctant to be honest, you can set an example. Throughout this discussion you'll need to be open to the possibility that some group member may have experienced a truly devastating loss that needs to be heard. At the same time, don't let someone's bitterness drag the group down. You'll need to discern the difference between grief and bitterness—and handle the group accordingly. This could be an opportunity for both the grieving and the bitter to receive God's healing.

Question 5. James was not writing from an ivory tower. He wrote out of the context of a church that had been racked with famine, poverty, and persecution. Believers whom he loved had been tortured and killed. He had personal experience with capital-T trials. Yet he was able to look beyond the trials to our good God, who was working out his good purposes.

Question 9. Be sure to reserve ten minutes to review your Purpose-Driven Group Agreement. The end of a study is a chance to evaluate what has been good and what could be improved on in your group. It's a time for some people to bow out gracefully and for others to recommit for a new season. If you're planning to go on to another study in the DOING LIFE TOGETHER series, session 1 of that study will reintroduce the agreement. You don't have to discuss it again then if you do so now.

Consider planning a celebration to mark the end of this episode in your group. You might share a meal, go out for dessert, or plan a party for your next meeting.

ABOUT THE AUTHORS

Brett and Dee Eastman have served at Saddleback Valley Community Church since July 1997, after previously serving for five years at Willow Creek Community Church in Illinois. Brett's primary responsibilities are in the areas of small groups, strategic planning, and leadership development. Brett has earned his Masters of Divinity degree from Talbot School of Theology and his Management Certificate from Kellogg School of Business at Northwestern University. Dee is the real hero in the family, who, after giving birth to Joshua and Breanna, gave birth to identical triplets—Meagan, Melody, and Michelle. Dee is the coleader of the women's Bible study at Saddleback Church called "The Journey." They live in Las Flores, California.

Todd and Denise Wendorff have served at Saddleback Valley Community Church since 1998. Todd is a pastor in the Maturity Department at Saddleback, and Denise coleads a women's Bible class with Dee Eastman called "The Journey." Todd earned a Masters of Theology degree from Talbot School of Theology. He has taught Biblical Studies courses at Biola University, Golden Gate Seminary, and other universities. Previously, Todd and Denise served at Willow Creek Community Church. They love to help others learn to dig into God's Word for themselves and experience biblical truths in their lives. Todd and Denise live in Trabuco Canyon, California, with their three children, Brooke, Brittany, and Brandon.

Karen Lee-Thorp has written or cowritten more than fifty books, workbooks, and Bible studies. Her books include *A Compact Guide to the Christian Life*, *How to Ask Great Questions*, and *Why Beauty Matters*. She was a senior editor at NavPress for many years and series editor for the LifeChange Bible study series. She is now a freelance writer living in Brea, California, with her husband, Greg Herr, and their daughters, Megan and Marissa.

SMALL GROUP ROSTER

Name	Address	Phone	E-mail Address	Team or Role	Church Ministry
Bill Jones	*7 Alvalar Street L.F. 92665*	*766-2255*	*bjones@aol.com*	*Socials*	*children's ministry*

Be sure to pass your booklets around the room the first night, or have someone volunteer to type the group roster for all members. Encourage group ownership by having each member share a team role or responsibility.

Name	Address	Phone	E-mail Address	Team or Role	Church Ministry

Doing Life Together series

BRETT & DEE EASTMAN; KAREN LEE-THORP;
DENISE & TODD WENDORFF

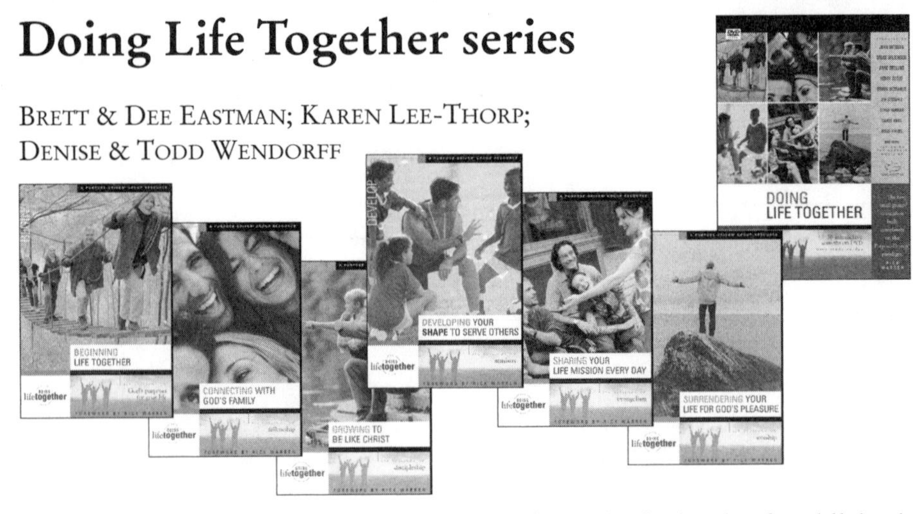

Based on the five biblical purposes that form the bedrock of Saddleback Church, Doing Life Together will help your group discover what God created you for and how you can turn this dream into an everyday reality. Experience the transformation firsthand as you begin Connecting, Growing, Developing, Sharing, and Surrendering your life together for him.

"Doing Life Together is a groundbreaking study ... [It's] the first small group curriculum built completely on the purpose-driven paradigm ... The greatest reason I'm excited about [it] is that I've seen the dramatic changes it produces in the lives of those who study it."

—FROM THE FOREWORD BY RICK WARREN

Small Group Ministry Consultation
Building a healthy, vibrant, and growing small group ministry is challenging. That's why Brett Eastman and a team of certified coaches are offering small group ministry consultation. Join pastors and church leaders from around the country to discover new ways to launch and lead a healthy Purpose-Driven small group ministry in your church. To find out more information please call 1-800-467-1977.

Curriculum Kit	ISBN: 0-310-25002-1
Beginning Life Together	ISBN: 0-310-24672-5 Softcover
	ISBN: 0-310-25004-8 DVD
Connecting with God's Family	ISBN: 0-310-24673-3 Softcover
	ISBN: 0-310-25005-6 DVD
Growing to Be Like Christ	ISBN: 0-310-24674-1 Softcover
	ISBN: 0-310-25006-4 DVD
Developing Your SHAPE to Serve Others	ISBN: 0-310-24675-X Softcover
	ISBN: 0-310-25007-2 DVD
Sharing Your Life Mission Every Day	ISBN: 0-310-24676-8 Softcover
	ISBN: 0-310-25008-0 DVD
Surrendering Your Life for God's Pleasure	ISBN: 0-310-24677-6 Softcover
	ISBN: 0-310-25009-9 DVD

ZONDERVAN™
GRAND RAPIDS, MICHIGAN 49530 USA
WWW.ZONDERVAN.COM